Speaking
and
Listening

for middle secondary students

Adrian Pauley
and
Kevin Ryan

PHOENIX EDUCATION

Speaking and Listening for Middle Secondary Students

First published in Australia in 2008
PHOENIX EDUCATION PTY L TD
PO Box 3141, Putney 2112
Tel: (02) 9809 3579
Fax: (02) 9808 1430
Email service@phoenixeduc.com

www.phoenixeduc.com

ISBN 978 1 921085 84 0

Cover design by Kate Stewart
Illustrations by Jane Reiseger
Printed in Australia by Five Senses Education

By the same authors

Speaking and Listening for junior secondary students
Speaking and Debating with Style

CONTENTS

CONTENTS (continued)

Chapter 1

Communication

Today, we communicate in so many different ways:

- **Written** – in letters, emails, sms, blogs
- **Spoken** – face-to-face with individuals and groups, telephone, voicemail
- **Multi-Media** – with video conferences, webpages

Students faced with this array of communication methodologies tend to willingly embrace those that are technology based; often to the detriment of the essential skills of listening and speaking face-to-face or to a group.

Verbal & Non-Verbal Messages

Whenever face-to-face communication takes place, it is taking place at three levels.

The message is conveyed both verbally (what is said) and non-verbally (how it is said). The non-verbal component can be further divided into visual and vocal components. In research originally done by Albert Mehrabian*, the relevant percentage for each component that contributed to the message was:

Verbal:	7%	The choice of words and their arrangement into phrases and sentences
Vocal:	38%	How the voice is used: rate, inflection, volume, tone, pause, emphasis
Visual:	55%	What the receiver sees: facial expressions, eye contact, gestures, stance, posture, dress & grooming, visual aids

Face-to-Face Communication

So, any face-to-face message is mostly being sent (and received) non-verbally. An appreciation of this helps students in many ways:

- As message receivers (listeners/observers) they better understand where the whole message is coming from.
- As message senders (in monologue and dialogue with individuals and groups) they better understand how they are putting their message out.

They can use this awareness whenever they are involved in face-to-face communication -

When in conversation:	By being aware of the message that their non-verbal communication is sending
When listening:	To listen as much with the eyes as the ears
When speaking to a group:	To think how non-verbal communication can be used to add to the impact of the message.

* Silent Messages by Albert Mehrabian (originally published 1970, republished 1980). At the time of writing, Albert Mehrabian is Emeritus Professor of Psychology at UCLA

exercises

1. Verbal Component: Discuss – are there any words/phrases that identify certain sub-groups, schools, areas, etc?
2. Vocal Component: Have students say aloud the phrase "*That's just what I need!*" It can be said both positively and negatively, so have them alternate.
3. Using a video of a conversation between two people (movie dialogue, television interview, etc) have students watch the first half and have the image obscured for the second half.

   Discuss which was easier to understand and why.

   Were the students aware of how much they relied on visuals to understand?

FACE-TO-FACE COMMUNICATION

People give and send face-to-face messages this way...

VERBAL The **words**, phrases & sentences	7%
VOCAL How the voice is used – *rate, inflection, volume, tone, pause & emphasis*	38%
VISUAL What the audience sees – *facial expressions, eye contact, gestures, stance, posture, dress & grooming, visual aids*	55%

How you can use this:

- **When in conversation**: Be aware of the message that non-verbal communication is sending.

  How you say a word and you're your facial expression when you say it both affect its meaning.

- **When listening**: Listen as much with your eyes as your ears.

- **When speaking to a group**: Think how non-verbal communication can be used to add to the impact of your message.

Chapter 2

Listening - What It Is

Hearing is no more than an awareness of a sound. It needs little effort. Listening, on the other hand, can be defined as hearing with the intent of understanding – and often requires considerable effort. To hear is defined as '*perceiving with the ear*' whereas to listen is described as '*to hear attentively*'.

HEARING An awareness of sounds perceived by the ears.	+	**CONCENTRATION** The conscious effort to understand the meaning of the sounds.	=	**LISTENING**

Listening is an active process with choices being made continuously by the listener. We often teach ourselves to 'tune out' sounds we might be hearing – because they are unpleasant or so we can concentrate on something else. For example…

Those who live near a railway line, a busy road or under a flight path soon do not notice the sound of the trains, traffic or planes. Everyone has had the experience of only becoming aware of a background noise (eg a noisy air conditioner) once it stops.

The Listening Process

This diagram shows the process that a listener will take in receiving a message.

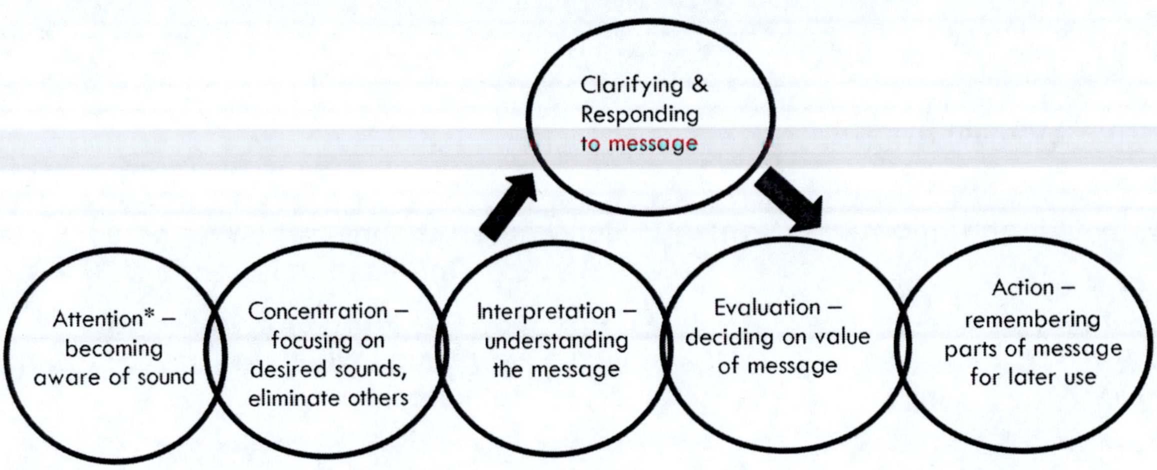

* *The first part of the message only serves as a 'switch-on' trigger. It is generally not actually heard well enough to be interpreted – this is why public address systems often have a 'pre-announce tone' to gain people's attention before the actual message is given.*

The process only continues if the listener makes the commitment to progress to the next step. Listeners are making these choices continually – and switching from one mode to the next. This switch is not always 'forward'. Often, a listener will 'downgrade' their listening level because they decide that the information is less useful to them or because something else has grabbed their attention.

The Message Package

Sending a message involves creating a 'package' that is able to travel the distance between the sender and the receiver. For the message to be successful, the 'package', when opened (heard) by the receiver, will accurately represent the intent of the sender.

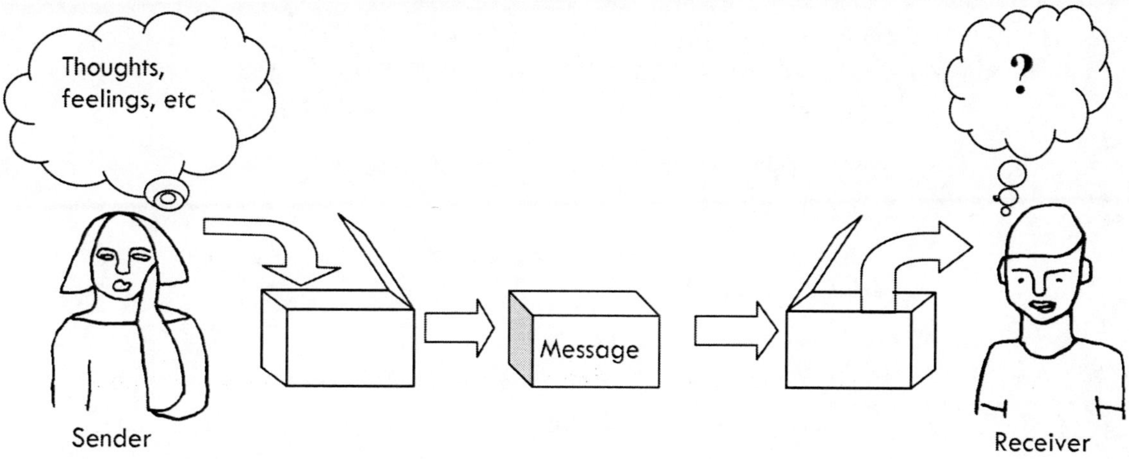

Message Variables

The message-sending process is subject to a large number of variables –

- The ability of the sender to create a message that accurately reflects what they want to say.
- The obstacles that the message has to overcome in-between sender and receiver.
- The ability and willingness of the receiver to accept the message as it is sent.

Message Components

A listener needs to be aware of the components of the message. As we know, any message, when sent, consists of three basic components –

Verbal Component 7%

Vocal Component 38%

Visual Component 55%

Listening on the telephone does not involve the visual component. This is compensated for mostly by the listener's heightened awareness of the vocal component:

Verbal Component 25%

Vocal Component 75%

exercises

The Visual Message Exercise

Put this question to students. Have them nominate the message they would take from this. They could work either as individuals or as pairs/threes.

While a speaker is talking to you, they regularly do one of the following. Describe what message you would interpret from this body language:

- *Constantly looks over your shoulder, just avoiding eye contact*
- *Frowns whenever they mention a certain person's name*
- *Smiles constantly at you*
- *When talking to you from a seated position, leans back and puts their hands behind their head*
- *Points their finger at you constantly*
- *Smiles and nods at you every so often*
- *Constantly stands in a slouched way, leaning against the desk*
- *Shrugs and shakes head whenever a certain name is mentioned*

What Listening Is - Information Sheet

HEARING
An awareness of sounds perceived by the ears.

+

CONCENTRATION
The conscious effort to understand the meaning of the sounds.

=

LISTENING

The Listening Process

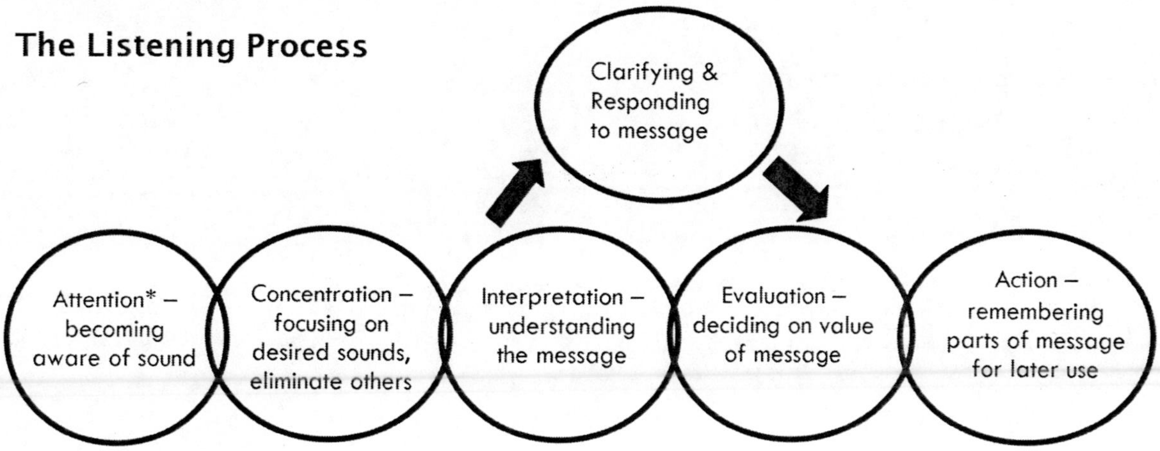

The Message Path

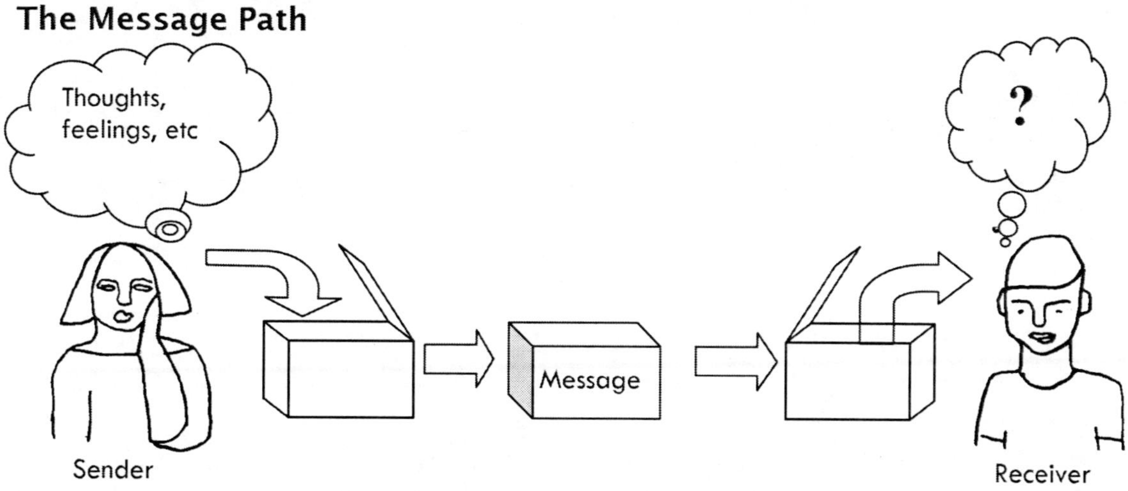

VARIABLES: Sender's Skills   Obstacles/Interference   Receiver's Skills

The Message Components

Verbal Components: Choice of words, phrase and sentence structure

Vocal Components: Volume, pace & tone of voice, articulation, use of pause & emphasis

Visual Components: Gestures, facial expressions, posture, eye contact

Chapter 3

Listening Filters

Filtering the Message

Listeners interpret every message through a 'filtering system'. This is based on a number of factors, some of which are:

- their existing knowledge of the topic
- their opinion of the sender
- their attitude to the topic
- their beliefs
- their life experience
- their personal needs

This filtering is an essential part of the listener's understanding and analysis of the message. Every listener's 'filter system' will be different – which means that they will all 'hear' a slightly different message.

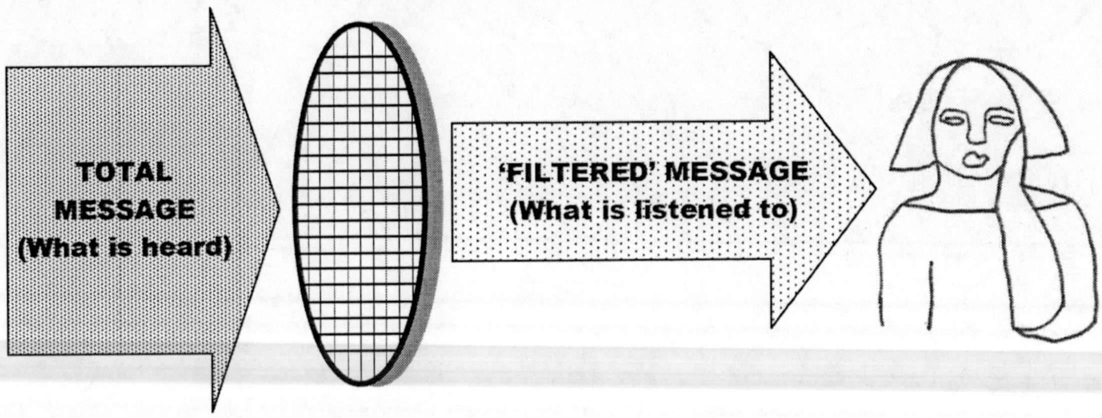

Knowledge of the Topic

How much a listener already knows about a topic significantly affects their listening level and the message that gets through. This can be in either a positive or negative way.

Positive

- Their existing knowledge of topic assists their understanding
- Their prior experience of topic assists their ability to evaluate the information

Negative

- Having prior knowledge can lead to 'know-it-all' attitude
- Being experienced can cause a listener to only accept the parts of the message that fit with their experience (narrow-mindedness)

Opinion of the Sender

Positive

- They may already know the sender, so the existing positive relationship makes them more inclined to listen.
- They may have heard of the speaker's expertise on this topic, which gives them the credibility to be listened to.

Negative

- They may have a negative opinion of the sender – based on past experience or reputation –causing them to reject the message.

Attitude to the Topic

Positive

- If they have a positive attitude to then topic, they are more inclined to listen.
- If they know little about the topic; but its benefits to them are made clear early, they will make the effort to listen.

Negative

- If they have a negative attitude to then topic, they are less inclined to listen – or to listen only to find fault.
- If they know little about the topic and its benefits are not made clear early, they will not make the effort to listen.

Beliefs

A listener's beliefs and values form part of the framework that allows them to understand and evaluate a message. It is important that a listener uses their beliefs and values as a filter, not a block – stopping what is uncomfortable to hear.

If a listener decides – on later evaluation of the message – that it is not valid or relevant based on their beliefs and values, then that is fine - as long as they have not stopped or unnecessarily modified the message getting through.

Life Experience

The life experience of a listener can impact on their willingness to listen. This may come in many forms:

- they perceive the message as being similar to previous experiences which turned out badly.
- the manner of the sender reminds them of someone they dislike
- they believe they've been misled in the past, so they are very skeptical and/or cynical

Personal Needs

All listeners listen for the answer to one essential question:

What is in this for me?

While it might seem negatively self-centred, it is an important part of the listening process – in deciding to upgrade or downgrade the listening. Nobody can listen to everything at the highest level – 'concentration exhaustion' would set in.

Switching levels is an essential listening skill – and the 'what's in this for me?' question is one of the most important triggers for this.

Staying Open-Minded

It is easy for our listening filters to become 'clogged-up' – so instead of assisting our understanding, they make us narrow-minded by inhibiting any content that challenges the status quo.

Here are three rules for staying open-minded:

1. **There's always more to know**

   In this fast moving world, information changes daily. What was correct last year could be totally wrong this year.

2. **Every situation is unique.**

   Even though you may have been involved in a very similar incident, remember that because the time, circumstances and people are different, it can never be exactly the same.

3. **Time changes (almost) everything**

   People change. Places change. Do not let your knowledge of what they were like in the past blind you to the fact that they may be totally different now.

exercises

Have students imagine they are listening to an expert deliver a lecture on how to deal with bush fires. This is of particular interest because they are about to spend a week doing work experience with the Country Fire Service – at the height of the fire season.

In small groups, have them consider the following factors and whether they would affect their willingness to listen.

- *Some students have recently finished a two month project on bush fires.*
- *Some students don't like the expert because of the way she dresses.*
- *Some students have fought bush fires at their own or friends' properties.*
- *Some students are very worried about the possibility fo bush fires.*
- *Some students think that bush fires are rare and they're unlikely to ever be affected.*
- *Some students think that bush fires play an important role in nature and shouldn't be stopped.*

Discuss their group responses about what would affect their listening and why.

Listening Filters

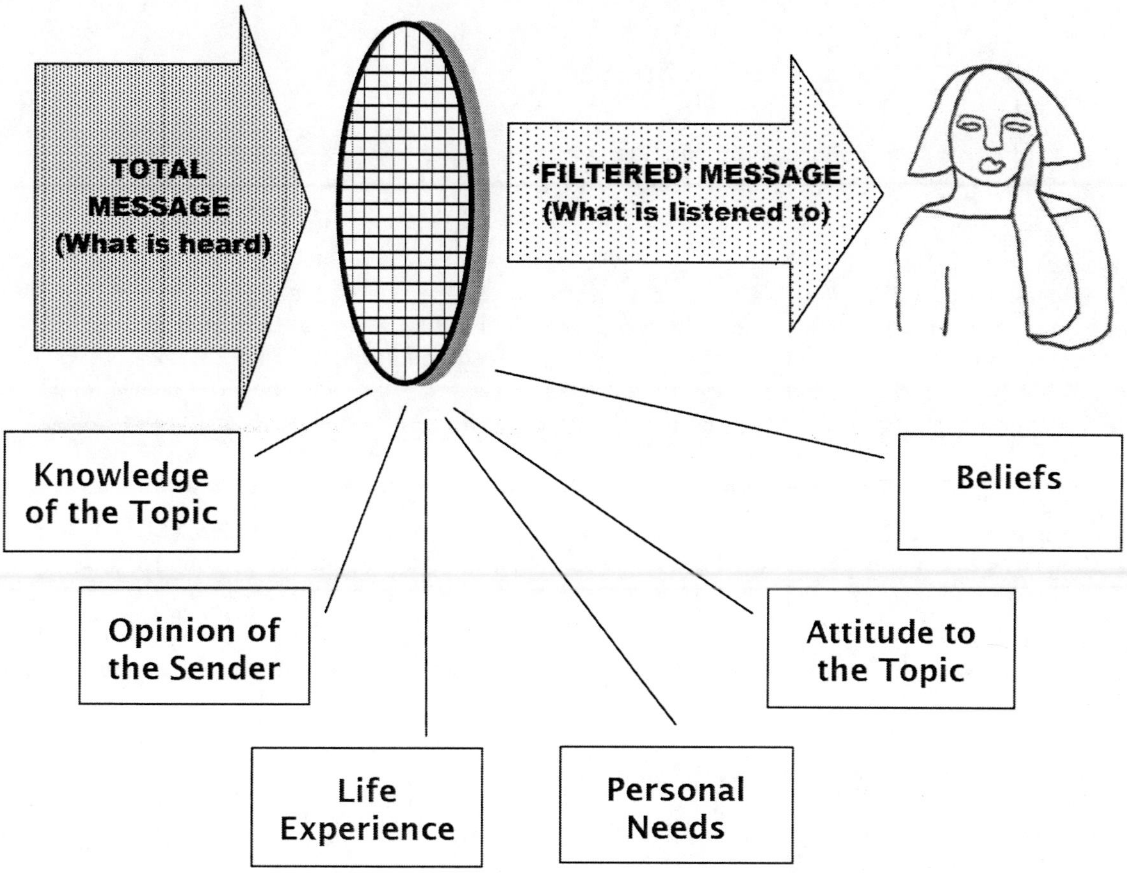

3 RULES for STAYING OPEN-MINDED

1 ***There's always more to know***

In this fast moving world, information changes daily. What was correct last year could be totally wrong this year.

2 ***Every situation is unique.***

Even though you may have been involved in a very similar incident, remember that because the time, circumstances and people are different, it can never be exactly the same.

3 ***Time changes (almost) everything***

People change. Places change. Do not let your knowledge of what they were like in the past blind you to the fact that they may be totally different now.

Chapter 4

Listening Requirements

Empathy

For listening to result in real understanding, the listener needs to have some empathy for the sender. Empathy is defined as 'mentally identifying oneself with a person' (Shorter Oxford Dictionary); but is probably best described by the saying "put yourself in their place."

This means that the listener needs to be able to relate to the speaker's emotions and circumstances to really understand what they are saying. It does not mean that the listener needs to have had the same experiences or felt emotions to the same depth – just that they have had sufficient life experience to have known something similar. For example, a young person who has not experienced the death of anyone close to them might think of the death of their pet animal when listening to someone speak of the death of their spouse of 50 years. While the two experiences are vastly different, the sense of loss and grief the young person felt at the death of the pet helped them empathise with and so better understand the speaker.

Some listeners avoid empathising – especially when they disagree with the sender and/or the message. They do this because they think it will somehow compromise them. It is important to stress: understanding does not have to mean the listener agrees with the speaker.

Empathizing with someone you agree with requires no effort at all...it probably happens naturally. Making the effort to empathise with someone we disagree with increases our understanding.

Suspended Judgement

We are constantly judging what we pay attention to. Listeners use their sense of judgement with everything they hear to:

- accept it completely and totally
- disregard it completely
- accept some of it and reject the rest.

Listeners will make this judgement based on a number of factors:

- their knowledge
- experience
- opinion of the sender
- attitude
- beliefs

and this judgement is part of the listening process – but it should be done at the end.

To listen effectively, it is necessary to defer this judgement until the sender has provided ALL the information. Otherwise, the listener makes a judgement based on insufficient information – and, then, uses this incorrect judgement as another filter to reject all or part of the message.

Awareness

Listeners need to be aware, not only of all the different components of the message, but also of the context in which it is being sent. Author Hugh Mackay (*The Good Listener*) said "*The message in what is said will be interpreted in the light of how when where and by whom it is said*".

Any message must be interpreted 'in context'. That is, the listener has to be aware of the following circumstances regarding the message –

When it is said

What are the prevailing circumstances? Are there any recent events that might have affected the message? Why did they choose this time to give this message?

Where it is said

Is there some significance of the place they chose to say it? Were there particular people present that the speaker wanted to get the message to?

Who said it

Was this the only person who could have given this message? If not, why was he or she chosen? What is this person's motivation for saying it?

Concentration

This is possibly the most difficult area to master – but without it all other listening skills are useless. With so many distractions competing for a listener's attention, simply being able to concentrate on what the other person is saying takes considerable effort. If listeners adhere to the following guidelines, they have the best chance of concentrating in a way that allows them to listen effectively.

Mental Focus

It is important to focus the mind on what the speaker is saying. Listeners need to make a conscious effort to 'shut out' any other issues that may be occupying their minds.

Listeners are tempted to think about what their response might be when the speaker has finished – when they should be putting all of their energy into hearing what the speaker has to say. While it is great to empathise with the speaker by thinking "*How would I feel if that happened to me?*" This should not be seen as an opportunity for the listeners to add their own stories. For example-

A person tells a story about a bad travel experience and the listener immediately responds with the story of his or her own 'travel disaster' tale.

Someone mentioning that they have just had a surgical procedure is guaranteed to have somebody else using the opportunity to re-tell the story of their operation.

These are generally characterised by a sort of 'one-upmanship' with the listener trying to outdo the speaker. ("*You think that was bad. Let me tell you about my experience!*" It is certainly very bad listening.

The listener should make a real effort to identify the speaker's message by looking for key points and consistent themes. This means thinking about the thoughts and emotions behind the words.

Physical Focus

If possible, listeners should use their eyes as much as their ears. Up to 55% of a speaker's message comes from the visual component – gestures, facial expression, etc. Visually focusing on the speaker makes it easier to ignore any possible distractions. It makes comprehension easier – particularly if the speaker's articulation and voice projection are lacking.

Body Language

The body language of a listener can affect their listening. Focusing the body helps to focus the mind. The listener should try to position themselves so that they are 'front-on' to the speaker. Fiddling, jiggling or unnecessarily moving about while the other person is talking should be avoided.

Sitting in an alert position assists the ability to concentrate.

For example, if you were to sit in an alert position watching an information TV show for an hour; then, the next day, watch a similar show while lying back in a comfortable armchair, you would notice that –

your ability to concentrate on the second show was less.

you remembered less of what you saw on the second show.

Relaxing back in a comfortable chair might feel great – but for anything other than relaxing (eg listening to music) it makes listening less efficient.

Evaluation

Messages come to us from all different sources – biased and unbiased, credible and not so credible. A skilled listener does not accept all that is heard as having the same value. This evaluation process is an important part of listening effectively.

The way the sender and context are evaluated and how this affects the message have been covered previously. This section is concerned with the evaluation of the arguments or points made.

The two most useful evaluations for a listener to make are:

- is it a fact?
- is it relevant?

Is It a Fact?

A skilled listener will question whether statements presented to them as facts are, in fact, true. They will make this assessment based on the available evidence, so they may decide one of the following:

"That's definitely a fact. It's been proven."

"That's probably true...based on the evidence available."

"That's difficult to prove; but I'm inclined to believe it's true."

"That's definitely not a fact. I know otherwise."

"That's being presented as a proven fact...but it' just an opinion."

Statements that are not facts tend to fall into one of the following categories.

- Opinions
- Generalisations and weeping statements are comments presented as being true but, in reality, go beyond the available evidence.
- Assumption is a judgement or opinion which is accepted as being true even if there is uncertainty about its truth.
- Deliberate and unintentional untruths

Is It Relevant?

Even if a statement is true, it isn't necessarily relevant in the context in which it is being used. For example, in the statement: "*We shouldn't let the year seven's use that area because they'll mess it up. In the last school I was in, the year seven area was always the messiest.*" The statement in the second sentence may well be true – but it's irrelevant. What occurred in the year seven area at another school has little to do with the situation at hand. The speaker is using an irrelevant fact to justify the assumption in the first sentence ("*...they'll mess it up.*").

exercises

Empathy

Have students imagine that they are in one of the following situations. Their task is to identify the real life experience they have had that might allow them to empathise with that speaker.

1. *A survivor of a Himalayan blizzard tells of how cold they were.*
2. *A member of the Australian cricket team talks about the day they were dropped from the team.*
3. *A visually impared person talking about the need for more aids for the blind at the airport.*
4. *A homeless person talking about life 'on the streets'.*
5. *A Gold Medal Olympic sports person telling of how it felt to win gold.*

Awareness

This exercise demonstrates that the same words said by different people in different situations can carry a totally different message. It is their awareness of the context that adds meaning. Have them consider the words: "*That's right. Keep doing it that way.*" What might the meaning be if said by these people:

1. *Your teacher*
2. *A student from the same year as you (or higher)*
3. *A student who is four years younger than you*
4. *A member of your team during a game*
5. *A member of the opposing team*
6. *A spectator at the game*

Evaluation

Have students consider the following statements. They are made by different people in a discussion about the colour of the new school hall. Students should rate each statement as either (1) Relevant Fact (2) Irrelevant Fact (3) Opinion, assumption, generalization, etc.

1. *All school buildings should be grey*
2. *People love pink.*
3. *Most school buildings throughout the country are grey.*
4. *More accidents happen in grey buildings than any other colour.*
5. *It's the first building people see when they arrive at the school.*
6. *Blue would look really impressive.*
7. *Some colours are more difficult to mark with graffiti.*

Listening Requirements

EMPATHY – “*Put yourself in their place.*”

Empathising with someone you agree with is **easy** and teaches you **nothing**.
Empathising with someone you disagree with is more difficult – but it teaches you **understanding**.

SUSPENDED JUDGEMENT –
Don’t judge until you’ve heard it all.

AWARENESS

When was it said?
Where was it said?
Who said it?

The same words in a different context can have the opposite meaning.

CONCENTRATION

Focus your mind
Empathise
Concentrate on the other person
Watch as well as listen
Focus your body
Face them, sit still

EVALUATION

Is it true?
Is it relevant?

Chapter 5

Active Listening Skills

Many of these techniques will already be used by students – but their use is arbitrary, imprecise, almost accidental. Describing the techniques and the times when they are most useful, helps listeners turn them into skills that they can actively use in their communication.

Encouragers

Encouragers are simply a verbal reassurance that you are still interested in what the other person is saying. They 'encourage' a listener to tell us more and so can facilitate more meaningful input from the sender. Encouragers are accompanied by positive body language – for example: expressions of interest on the face, nodding, leaning forward.

The tone of voice is very important, for example: saying "*really?*" in an interested or surprised tone of voice is a great encourager. The same word said in a dry, sarcastic tone has the meaning "*I couldn't care less.*"

Encouragers tend to be more prevalent at the start of a conversation, but are used throughout – especially where there is no visual contact (as in a telephone conversation). A lot of the time, they are nothing more than "*uh-huh*" or just one word. Sometimes, they consist of a phrase or sentence.

Examples	*hmmm*	*uh-huh*
	wow	*okay*
	great	*I see*
	oh no	*you're kidding*
	that's interesting	*tell me more*

Summarising the Content

This allows the listener to check that they have understood by reflecting back to the speaker the content (facts) of what has been said. The listener uses the same words as the speaker with the intention of being confident that all the important points have been noted as well as checking that nothing has been missed.

This helps the listener to concentrate by separating the salient facts from the trivia.

It needs to be done with discretion – too much can interrupt the flow of information.

Example

Initial Statement:

"*You won't believe what we did for the last week of the holidays. First we went on a yacht around the islands for three days, then we stayed in this fantastic resort – four days and they had heaps of great things to do.*"

Reflecting Content:

"*So it sounds like the last week of your holidays was spent in the lap of luxury – first the boat, then the resort.*"

Paraphrasing

This is an advancement on summarising the content because it uses **the listener's own words.** It has the advantage of being much more concise. It also avoids any misunderstanding caused by two people having different interpretations of the same word. The speaker may 'correct' the listener's paraphrase and this should not be seen as negative. On the contrary, it is a sign that real communication is taking place.

Summarising Content and **Paraphrasing** are closely related skills. The definition of the skill being used is not important; rather that listeners apply them as needed to clarify the content of what the speaker is saying.

Example

Initial Statement:

"You won't believe what we did for the last week of the holidays. First we went on a yacht around the islands for three days, then we stayed in this fantastic resort – four days and they had heaps of great things to do."

Paraphrase:

"So your holidays ended on a high!"

Reflecting Feelings

Probably the most advanced of the listening skills, this requires the listener to assess the combination of content, vocal use, body language, prior knowledge of the speaker and many other factors and nominate the feeling of either how the speaker feels now or felt in the past. A listener usually interprets this based on –

- what the speaker says about how they feel
- how you think they might feel
- how the listener would feel in the same situation

Example

Initial Statement

"You won't believe what we did for the last week of the holidays. First we went on a yacht around the islands for three days, then we stayed in this fantastic resort – four days and they had heaps of great things to do."

Reflection of Feelings

"You must have felt excited when you found out you were going on a yacht."

OR

"You must feel exhausted after doing so much."

This skill makes for much better communication because it takes the speaker beyond the facts into their feelings about the situation.

Questioning

Questions can fall into two broad categories: closed and open

Closed Questions

These are questions that generally require a yes or no answer. They are best for clarifying specific facts or issues.

Examples

"Did you go on the yacht with your family?"

"Was the weather good?"

Open Questions

These are the opposite to closed questions in that they cannot be answered with a yes or no. They are used to encourage the speaker to expand on a topic and are characterised by words such as how, who, what, when, where, why.

Examples

"Who did you go on the yacht with?"

"What was the weather like?"

Open questions, simply because they cannot be answered with a yes or a no, tend to draw the speaker out – encouraging them to share more information.

Asking of questions takes a little care because to ask a question as soon as it occurs to you will often mean interrupting the speaker – which should only be done as a last resort. For example, when something the person has said is so confusing it is stopping your understanding of the conversation.

Questions are meant to help us to understand the speaker, to let them know that we are interested and to encourage them to share more information. Too many questions can turn a conversation into an interrogation.

exercises

Summarising Content

Have students summarise the content of each of the following sayings in no more than two sentences. They could do this as individuals, pairs or small groups.

1. *"You should see the costume I have to wear for the school play. It takes me half an hour to put it on, it's made of about fifteen layers of fabric and plastic, and it weighs a ton. I need two helpers just to get from the dressing room onto the stage!"*
2. *"Our new house is just great. Every bedroom has its own telephone, cable TV and internet access. We've all got computers. The only trouble is our parents have decided it's best to limit the amount of time we can use them. "*
3. *"I've had such a lousy day. First, my Mum told me off for leaving the milk out of the fridge overnight, then the bus driver didn't want to let me on the bus because I accidentally threw away this week's ticket and kept last week's, then my teacher gave me detention for being late with an assignment."*

Paraphrasing

Using the same statements as in the **Summarising Content Exercise,** paraphrase them in one sentence.

Reflecting Feelings

Imagine you are in a conversation with another student. For each of the following statements, write a Reflection of Feelings that you might respond with.

1. *"All our family is going to Disneyland in the school holidays. Going to America is something I've always wanted to do! It'll be great – I can't wait!"*
2. *"Do you know what my little brother just did? He erased all of my last week's work off the computer to make space for his new game. I could kill him!"*
3. *"The final exam in this subject is only three weeks away. There's no way I can catch up in that time. I don't know what to do."*
4. *"My best friend's family is going skiing for the weekend and they've asked me to go. I'd love to, but I'd set aside this weekend to catch up on my assignment."*
5. *"Rover, our eighteen year beagle, died in his sleep last night. I'm really going to miss him, but in a way, it's a relief because he was suffering terribly from arthritis and we couldn't do any more to ease the pain."*

Use this list of feelings for the **Reflecting Feelings Exercise**.

amazed	*delighted*	*guilty*	*regretful*
anxious	*disappointed*	*horrified*	*relieved*
angry	*disapproving*	*hopeful*	*sad*
apologetic	*disgusted*	*jealous*	*satisfied*
apprehensive	*ecstatic*	*lonely*	*shocked*
bitter	*embarrassed*	*loved*	*strong*
cautious	*enthusiastic*	*meditative*	*surprised*
concerned	*envious*	*mischievous*	*suspicious*
confident	*excited*	*miserable*	*sympathetic*
content	*exhausted*	*obstinate*	*tense*
confused	*frightened*	*optimistic*	*thoughtful*
curious	*frustrated*	*perplexed*	*threatened*
determined	*grieving*	*proud*	*worried*

Questioning

1 Nominate which of the following questions are open and which are closed.

1 *Has the next train been delayed?*

2 *What movie would you like to see?*

3 *Would you like to see a movie?*

4 *Will we be meeting many people?*

5 *Do you like the red one?*

6 *What colours do you like in this?*

7 *Who will we be meeting?*

8 *Did you go to Rocky Island?*

9 *Where did you go on the yacht?*

10 *Why has the train been delayed?*

Change the closed questions in this list into open questions.

1 *Do you like hamburgers?*

2 *Did you ride the roller-coaster?*

3 *Do you think this suits me?*

4 *Did you like the movie?*

5 *Are you a good swimmer?*

6 *Do you think that the price is important?*

7 *Do they have a big range of shoes?*

8 *Will it take long to get there?*

exercises

Active Listening Skills

Encouragers

- Tell a speaker that you are paying attention
- Encourage them to keep speaking - tell you more

Examples	*hmmm*	*uh-huh*	*oh no*
	wow	*okay*	*that's interesting*
	great	*I see*	*you're kidding*
		cool	*tell me more*

Summarising the Content

- Deals with the facts of what the speaker says
- Condenses the speaker's words - concentrating on the main points
- Allows you to check that you have understood the important details

Paraphrasing

Similar to *Summarising Content*, but uses your own words - eliminates chances of misunderstanding caused by different interpretation of the same word.

Shorter than *Summarising Content* - less chance of interrupting the speaker

Reflecting Feelings

Looks beyond the content of what a speaker says: concentrates on how they feel about it.

Interpreted through a combination of -

- what the speaker says about how they feel
- how you think they might feel
- how you would feel in the same situation

Encourages the speaker to share their feelings with you

Questions

Closed questions: answered with a '*yes*' or '*no*'

Good for checking details, clarifying specifics

Open questions: cannot be answered with a "*yes*' or '*no'*

Often use '*how*', '*what*', '*why*', '*when*', '*where*', '*who*'

Good for encouraging speaker to give more information

Chapter 6

Conversation Skills – the '*what*'

Conversation, like all face-to-face communication, can be divided into:

- the verbal component – what is said
- the non-verbal component – how it is said

This section is dedicated to the '*what*' of conversation. Although research has shown that the verbal component contributes less to the communication than the non-verbal, it is a mistake to believe it is unimportant. In fact, the identification of a suitable topic is the forerunner to most successful conversations

Common Ground

A common complaint that many people make when trying to hold a conversation with someone they don't know well is, "*I don't know what to talk about.*" Once you have been able to find something that you have in common with the other person, conversation becomes much easier. Finding this 'common ground' is a skill that can be developed. This 'common ground' can be divided into four different levels. These are generally indicative of the strength of the connection.

Situational

The situational level is the first and shallowest level. It exists between any two people standing together. They share the same weather or inside temperature; they share the same space and situation, for example, a bus, a supermarket aisle, waiting in a queue. These are often the most banal of topics, but they are the starting point of most conversations between strangers because they are safe. No personal disclosure is required. If the conversation continues, it will probably progress to one of the other levels.

Circumstantial

This level is where you share similar circumstances. Generally, these are life circumstances about which you have had no choice.

- Family situation: you come from similar sized families, perhaps single-parent or blended families; you have a big/little brother/sister of similar age.
- Abilities/Talents: You're good at the same subjects or sports.
- School Situation: You're in the same year and/or house, you have the same teachers, you went to the same primary school
- Experiences: You've had similar life experiences: For example, moving from one city to another, changing schools, school camps.
- Problems/Concerns: You worry about exams, you both think that your parents are too strict.

Preferential

This is based on factors about which you have made a choice – your personal preferences. It is at this level that genuinely good conversations happen – where both (or all) parties are truly interested in the proceedings.

- Interests and hobbies
- Habits and practices – for example, fitness, procrastination, sleeping-in
- Subject preferences
- Likes and tastes – for example, music, books, movies
- Goals – academic, sporting, lifestyle, family

Core

These are your core values and passions. Many meaningful conversations will never make it to this level. If it is reached, it is a sign of trust on behalf of both parties.

These four levels have been combined on the 'Connection Wheel' which can be used by students to help them find the 'common ground' in conversation.

The Connection Wheel

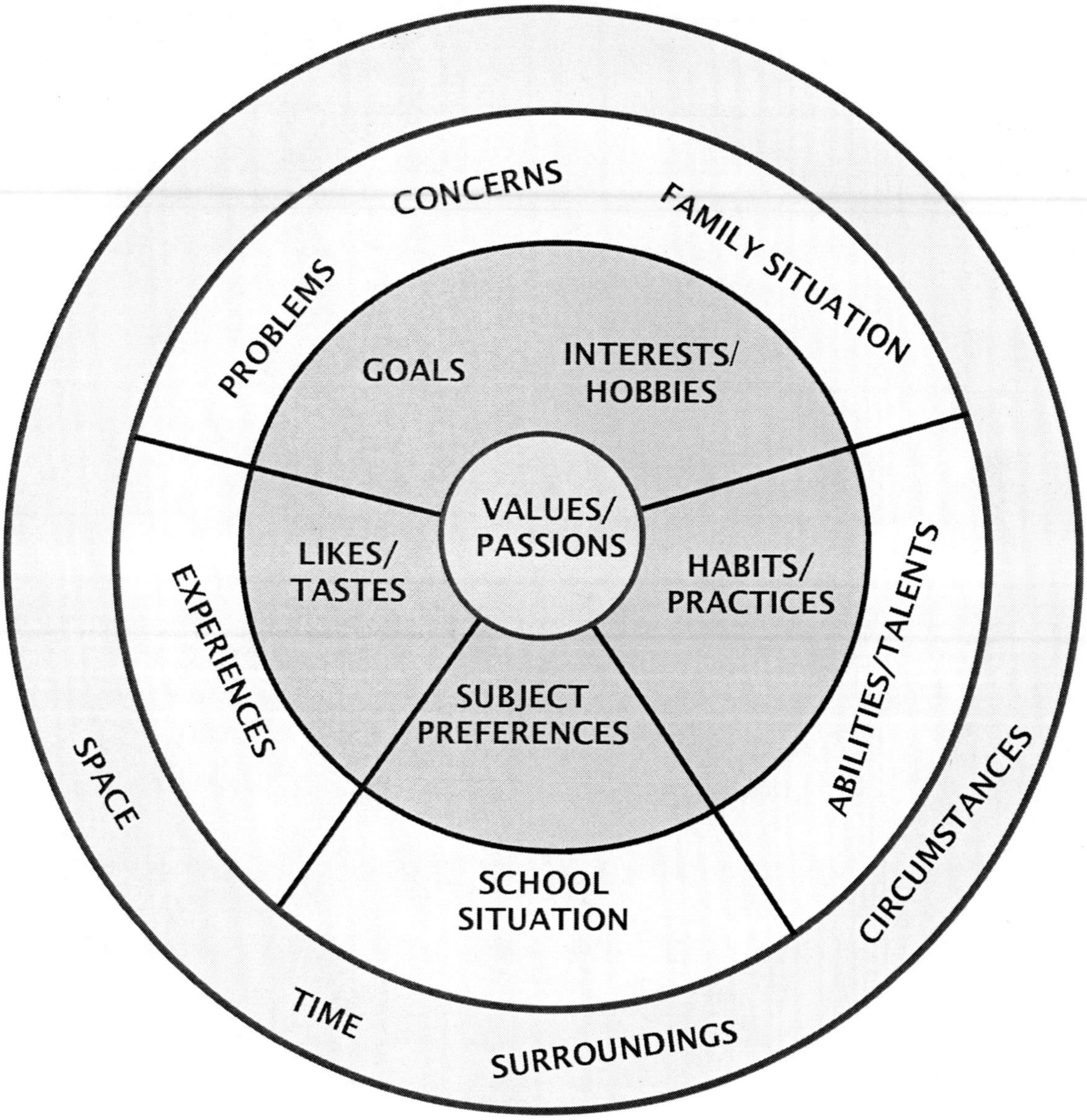

exercises

This is a pairs exercise, where students spend two minutes in a pair, then one moves on to form new pairs. It might best be done with two concentric circles, like a progressive barn dance.

In two minutes, the students in each pair must find common ground at the third or preferential level. They are to use open questions to identify their areas in common.

If the students know each other very well, you can increase the challenge by specifying that the common ground must be something that they previously didn't know about each other.

CONVERSATION SKILLS
The 'What'

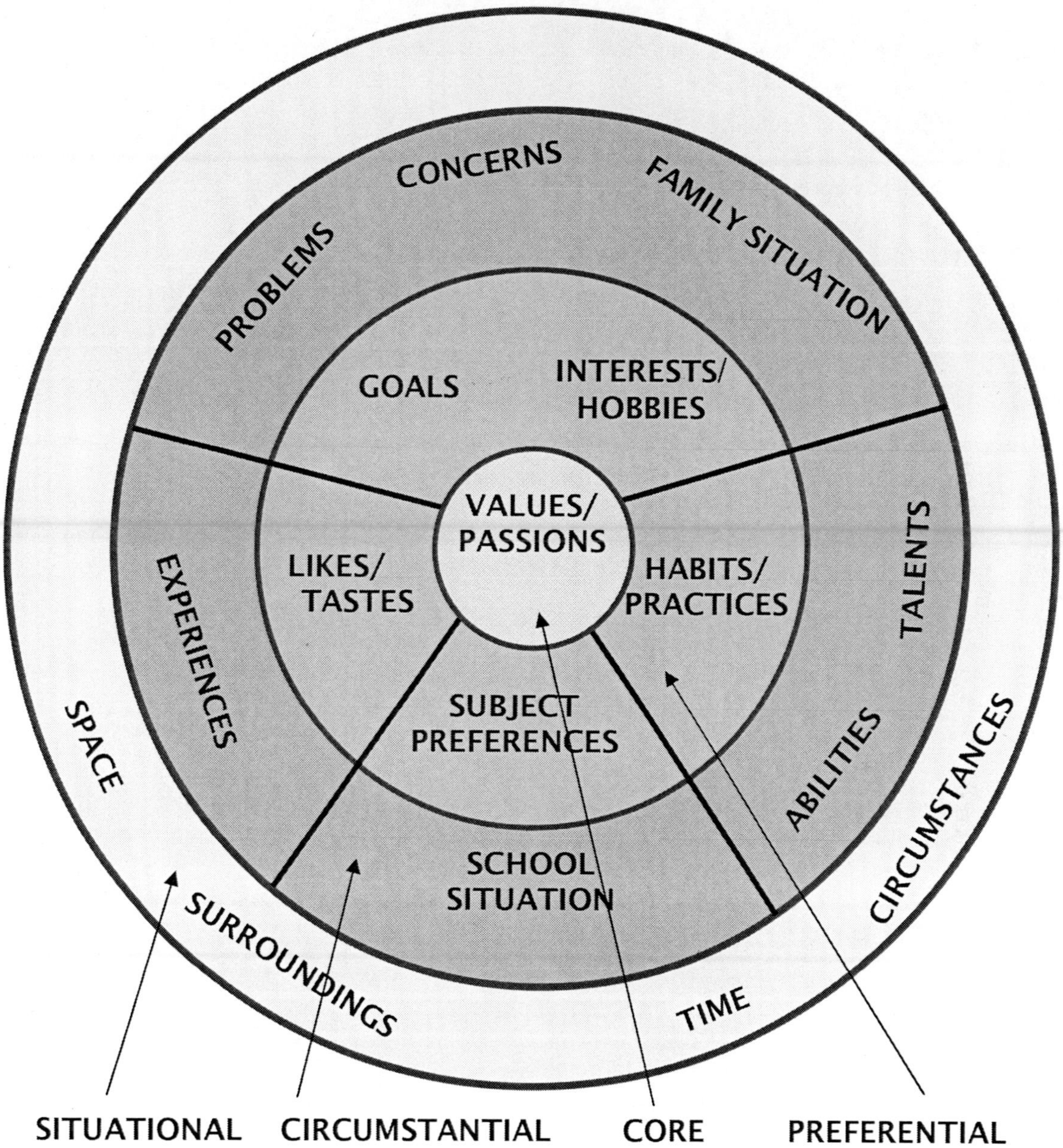

Situational	You share the same place and time
Circumstantial	You share the same life circumstances
Preferential	You share the same preferences, likes and dislikes
Core	You share the same life values

The sooner you can identify common ground with another person, the easier you will be able to maintain a conversation with them.

Chapter 7

Conversation Skills – The 'How'

Having looked at what a conversation might be about, it is now time to look at how that conversation is conducted. This 'how' of the conversation is evident in three areas:

1 the vocal content
2 the body language
3 the choice and use of language

Matching the Manner

When you observe a good conversation, you will notice that there is a certain 'matching' or 'mirroring' of the way each person is communicating. This will be happening without conscious effort by either party – they are simply making communication easier.

For those who wish to improve their conversation skills, an awareness of the other person's communication processes is important for two reasons –

1 Because up to 93% of the communication we receive is non-verbal, making an effort to concentrate on how something is being said and the body language that accompanies it results in much better understanding. When we listen for the vocal content rather than just the verbal; and when we listen with our eyes as much as our ears – we become better listeners.

2 Being aware of the other person's communication processes means that you are able to modify yours (if necessary) to facilitate the conversation. A good example of this would be when one speaker leans forward toward the other and they reciprocate. It's not about mimicking the other person. It's about matching their style so the conversation flows more easily.

A good conversation can be compared to two people walking together. They make an effort to walk side-by-side. They talk at similar levels. This provides a connection that makes communication possible.

The Vocal Content

To identify the vocal content, a student needs to listen for the way the other person uses their voice. This has been credited with carrying 38% of the message. The way that something is said can completely change the context – even the meaning – of the words used. For example, the phrase "*Yeah, right*" can be said in a positive, affirming way; or, it can be said with heavy sarcasm where the meaning is the exact opposite.

Tone

So much meaning comes from the tone of voice. When listening, think about what emotion is being shown (in their voice) when they speak about different topics.

Pauses/Gaps

Each person in a conversation should listen for the pauses or gaps used by the other person. They may be long and thoughtful or almost. If one person's gaps are longer than the other's, care is required for one not to cut the other off. One thinks they've finished speaking, so they take up the dialogue; but the other feels they've been interrupted.

Pace

It is easy for a 'fast' talker to become frustrated with a 'slow' talker – even to the point of finishing their sentences for them. This, obviously, makes conversation difficult.

Volume

Match the other's volume. If one person lowers their voice, the other should lower theirs out of respect. They may be about to share a confidence.

Body

The four main aspects of body language are:

1. Eye Contact

Is their eye contact really direct (retina-to-retina) and intense, or is it more indirect? Do they become uncomfortable with eye-to-eye contact; preferring to make the eye contact via an object and/or image? (For example, when two people are talking about something in front of them, and they are both looking at it as they talk.)

2. Position/Movement

Do they tend to lean forwards when they speak, or are they more 'laid back'? If they lean forward, it should be matched to show interest.

Do they tend to move around a lot – or sit still? Are their movements fast and expansive or slower and smaller? If they tend to stay still and move slowly, they are going to find it difficult to converse with a jittery, fast, over-the-top style.

3. Personal Space

Personal space is divided into three areas – anything else is 'public' space. The space perceptions in Western cultures are, on average –

Intimate space	Less than .5 metre
Personal space	.5 – 1.25 metres
Social space	1.25 – 3.5 metres
Public space	Greater than 3.5 metres

Different cultures require different personal spaces. This is most obvious with those from heavily populated areas (eg Japan and India) where less personal space is available. Even within the same culture, you will notice a difference between those from an urban and rural background.

The point is, you can quickly assess a person's personal space requirements – most obviously by seeing how much space they give others. The distance between conversationalists may change. For example, you will notice speakers move closer to each other as the topic of conversation moves from general topics to something more personal (from 'circumstantial' to 'preferential' on the Connection Wheel).

Language

A person's choice of words – and the way they string them together – carries much meaning. Matching language is something we do instinctively. Notice how quickly we adopt phrases from our friends and colleagues.

1. Detail

Does their conversation contain lots of detail? If so, they like that level of detail when information is shared with them.

2. Mode

Do they start most sentences with "...*I think.*?" or "*I feel*?". This can indicate whether their primary perceptions and reactions are based on logical thought or emotions.

Formality/Familiarity

Is their language 'formal' or more relaxed? Are they addressing you as someone in or out of their 'inner circle'? Do they use any particular jargon or slang? Matching the level of formality or familiarity is recommended. Matching jargon or slang should only happen if you are totally familiar with the genre – otherwise it will sound false and artificial.

Wordiness

Are their sentences long and detailed or short and clipped? This is one area where matching facilitates conversation.

In all these areas, the matching is done by both parties. For example with a slow and fast speaker, one would lift their pace while the other would slow down. Generally, the only reason it is not done is through lack of awareness. Sometimes, however, it is used as a bullying or disorienting technique by manipulative individuals.

exercises

Vocal Content

1. Choose a 3-5 minute section of dialogue from a radio play, audio book or similar. Have students identify what emotions are being demonstrated by each speaker. If appropriate, you could ask them to identify what aspect of the vocal content indicated each emotion. (For example, tone of voice, emphasis of a certain word, changed rate)
2. Have students work in pairs. Ask them to converse for 2 minutes (nominate the topic if you wish). Then have them compare themselves according to these criteria –
   - Compared to me, I think he/she speaks slower/faster/at the same rate.
   - Compared to me, I think he/she speaks louder/softer/at the same volume.
   - Compared to me, I think the pauses he/she uses are longer/shorter/the same length.

Body Language

1. Choose a 3-5 minute section of dialogue from a movie or television. Have students identify what emotions are being demonstrated by each speaker – and what body language indicated these emotions.
2. Have students work in pairs, sitting facing each other. Have them make eye contact and give them permission to break that eye contact as soon as it feels uncomfortable. After a few seconds, they are to make eye contact again – and break it as soon as it feels uncomfortable. The students are to note who is the first to break each time. It is important to make the point that this is an awareness exercise – not a staring contest. Holding eye contact for longer does not make you the winner. It is simply for students to become aware of their personal preference.
3. Have students stand in pairs. Ask them to move closer to each other until they feel that the other person has 'invaded' their personal space. Again, there is no right or wrong. It is not better or worse to prefer less/more personal space. It is for students to become aware of what their preference is.
4. Have students sit opposite each other in pairs having a conversation (with the topic provided if you wish). At different times have them move positions as follows –
   - With both students leaning back in their chairs
   - With one student leaning forward and their partner leaning back
   - With both students leaning forward

Have them comment on how the different positions affected the communication. (i.e. which was easiest/most difficult)

exercises

Language

1. Choose a 3-5 minute section of dialogue from a radio play, audio book, movie or television. Have students respond to these questions with respect to each of the characters –

   Did they like speaking in a lot of detail? Would you say they used lots of words or few words?

   Did they mainly talk about what they thought or what they felt?

   Did they talk to the other person like a stranger/acquaintance/colleague/friend/family member

1. Have students sit opposite each other in pairs having a conversation (with the topic provided if you wish). After 3-5 minutes have them write down their responses to these questions about their partner –

   He/she seems to like more/the same/less detail than I prefer.

   He/she seems to speak mostly about what they think/feel.

   I felt he/she spoke to me like I was a stranger/friend

   He/she seems to like to speak using more/less/the same words I do.

Conversation Skills

The 'How'

VOCAL CONTENT

Tone *What emotion is the person feeling?*

Pauses *Do they speak with short or long pauses?*
Have they finished what they want to say – or are they just gathering their thoughts?

Pace *What rate do they speak at?*
Can I match it?

Volume *Do they talk loudly or softly? Does it change?*

BODY LANGUAGE

Eye Contact *Do they make regular direct eye-contact – or is it more indirect?*

Personal Space *What personal space do they feel comfortable with?*
Is it the same as you? More/Less?

Position/ *Are they leaning forward/back/neutral?*

Movement *Do they move a lot? How quickly do they move?*

Volume *Do they talk loudly or softly? Does it change?*

LANGUAGE

Detail *Do they use a lot of detail – or little?*

Mode *Is their main focus "I think..." or "I feel..."?*

Formality/ Familiarity *Are they talking to you like a stranger / acquaintance / colleague / friend?*

Chapter 8

Speaking to a Group

Speaking in public has always been one of the greatest human fears. It has been estimated that up to 40% of people would rather die than attempt it. Like many fears, it is largely based on ignorance – basic ignorance of what constitutes a successful presentation and what is necessary to prepare for this.

How an Audience 'Hears' a Speaker

An audience listening to a speaker receives the message the same way as in all face-to-face communication:

7%	**The Verbal Component:**	The words and how they're combined into phrases and sentences
38%	**The Vocal Component:**	How the words are said
55%	**The Visual Component:**	What they are seeing while the speaker is talking

The exact percentages will obviously vary, but the undeniable fact is that a large percentage of the message is conveyed by methods other than just the words - how these words are said and what the audience is seeing while they are being said is also very important.

Preparing - The Right Way

Many speakers spend most of their preparation time working on the words alone. The components that contribute so much to their message, that is their vocal usage and their body language, happen by accident. This will result in a feeling of being unprepared – no matter how much time is spent on the words.

This does not mean that they should give less time to speech writing – just more time on the components which are generally ignored:

- how they will say it.
- what the audience will see while they are delivering it.

Avoiding Mixed Messages

Speakers give mixed messages when their non-verbal behaviour does not reflect what they say. For example, if a speaker were to say 'I'm really enjoying speaking to you' but the audience hears mumbling speech and sees them fidgeting nervously, they are unlikely to be convinced.

Mostly, mixed messages are caused by lack of preparation. If they'd had a 'run through' in front of a mirror beforehand, they would have seen the nervous gestures they needed to avoid. If they had said the line aloud in advance they would have had more confidence saying it to an audience.

Controlling Nervousness

Speakers generate a great deal of unnecessary nervousness. When standing in front of a group of people, it is very easy to convince oneself that every audience member is judging you - just waiting for you to make a mistake. Nervousness is quite normal. It can be overcome to a large extent if you remember the following points:

- Nervousness is natural. Eliminating it altogether is probably impossible but it can be controlled. In fact, eliminating nerves entirely would probably not be desirable just as an athlete expects to be a bit nervous before a big race.
- Be convinced by and care about your message. Not all speeches lend themselves to this, but for those that do it can help. The principle is that the more we care about the audience really getting our message, the less we focus on what they are thinking of us. Previously shy presenters can lose all nervousness when speaking to an audience about something they care about deeply.

Just Before Speaking

Breathing

Proper oxygenation is essential to speak to any group. The natural anxiety that most experience just before presenting tends to restrict breathing even more.

Before presenting, a speaker should be doing slow deep breathing.

This will have three effects –

1 It will give the lungs the air they need to properly project the voice.

2 It will give the brain the oxygen it needs to function effectively.

3 It will counteract the anxious 'racing' of the mind. Slowing down the body has the effect of slowing down the mind.

Water

Apart from oxygen, the body and mind need water. A speaker should aim to always have a glass of water with them while waiting to speak and another near the speaking position. Make sure it is cool to room temperature – definitely not iced water which will cause the vocal folds to contract. If all else fails, they should carry their glass of water with them to the speaking position.

This water can be used for two purposes –

1 Some speakers have their mouth go dry; or experience an urge to cough. In these cases, a sip of water will assist.

2 Taking a sip of water provides an effective 'circuit breaker' if you find your mind (and your mouth) racing or you are momentarily lost for words.

Mentally

In the five minutes before speaking, it is easy for performance nerves to get the better of you; allowing your mind to conjure up all sorts of negative scenarios. The adrenalin rush can cause some speakers to speak too quickly – destroying the impact of their opening. This is why it's important to focus on the message you want them to get and why it is important to them.

Starting Speaking

Controlled eye-contact

When speaking to a group, you should aim to have as much control as possible over the first part of your presentation. When you are saying your first words, it will help your confidence enormously if the eye-contact and body language that you receive from the audience members is interested, positive and encouraging. You can arrange this by choosing the 3-4 people (depending on the size of the group) that you will look at in the first part of your presentation. Select them before you speak, know where they are in the room as you make your way to the speaking position and look at them until you feel confident enough to look at others where the reaction is not so certain.

exercises

Have students practice deep breathing as is recommended in the five minutes before they speak

Conduct the exercise this way:

- *have them breathe slowly in to while you count to five*
- *have them hold it while you count to four*
- *have them breathe slowly out while you count to five*

Speaking Basics

When you speak, the message comes from -

THIS MUCH FROM WHAT YOU SAY

THIS MUCH FROM HOW YOU SAY

THIS MUCH FROM WHAT THE AUDIENCE SEES

You need to prepare

what you will say
how you will say it
what you want the audience to **see** while you say it.

Hints for the five minutes just before you speak...

Concentrate on the **main message** that you want to say.
Take slow, deep breaths before you start your speech.
Try to have water nearby to sip if you need.

Chapter 9

The Purpose

There are several steps in the preparation of any spoken presentation. These steps include:

- determining the **purpose** of the presentation
- deciding on the **message** the audience will remember
- choosing an **original approach**

What is the Purpose of the Presentation?

The first task to establish is what is expected of the presentation. It might be an assignment with clear assessment criteria and if so these should be examined.

The purpose might be to:

- inform
- persuade
- reflect or reminisce
- promote discussion
- provide a personal opinion (as in a review of a poem, play, etc)
- entertain
- inspire
- demonstrate knowledge

If in doubt, students should always be encouraged to ask because it is important to know what the presentation has to achieve before any other preparation is done.

What is the Message?

There will be some presentations where this is not appropriate; but, wherever possible, having a clear, succinct message should be encouraged. The purpose of introducing this so early in the process for students is two-fold –

1 If decided on before a student undertakes the information gathering, it will be much easier to judge what content will fit and what will not.

2 It will avoid the tendency that most students have of creating 'waffly', un-focused presentations with an over-abundance of unconnected information.

The message of a presentation should be able to be said in one short sentence. This is an excellent 'rule-of-thumb'. If a presentation fails this test, it is likely it will be too unfocused for the speaker to deliver powerfully and too complex for the audience to follow or remember.

Choosing an Original Approach

Students should be encouraged to use spoken presentations as an opportunity to demonstrate their originality. One way to do this is in the approach they choose.

This approach will be determined by:

- the purpose
- the audience and the occasion - e.g. a humorous approach would probably not be appropriate for a speech about youth suicide.

The speaker's own skills and personality have a lot of bearing on which approach is chosen. Some possible approaches are listed below, but this list is only a sampling. Sharing these with students can be an excellent 'idea-starter'. They might choose to use one or a combination of many techniques to develop a unique approach.

Dramatisation or Role Play

Re-creating an event dramatically can be very effective if the speaker wants the audience to empathise with a particular person or group of people. It allows the involvement of a wide range of emotions, particularly if the speaker is able to effectively set the scene - and place the audience in it.

Documentary

A logical, easy to understand way of describing an event or process - particularly if it involves complicated detail. It is very effective if the primary purpose is to inform.

Humorous

Humour includes many different styles - satire, slapstick, word-play etc. As long as it is handled tastefully and used in context, humour can be used in almost any situation. It can offer a non-threatening way of tackling difficult, sensitive subjects, or a more interesting approach to what might be considered a 'dull' subject.

The Allegorical Approach

This is the method used by the great fable writers like Aesop and Hans Christian Andersen; for example: using animal stories to parallel human behaviour. Comparing and contrasting that which you wish to speak about to something familiar to your audience adds originality and interest.

exercises

For these exercises, use a typical presentation that students will have to give this year. If this is impractical, you can use a hypothetical example such as 'World Cup Football'.

Determine the Purpose

You can determine the purpose, or you may decide to allow students to choose. This could be one of the following:

- Inform students about the World Cup competition
- Persuade them that it is worth following
- Review the last World Cup competition (or preview the upcoming one)
- Promote discussion about how this compares to other international contests (eg the Olympics)
- Provide a personal insight into what they find appealing about the World Cup
- Demonstrate their knowledge of the contest – its history, rules, traditions, etc

Deciding on the Message

Their next step is to decide on the message that they want everyone to remember from their talk – that is, if the audience were to be asked at the end of the talk "*What was that all about?*", this is what they would say.

The one topic can have many different messages, and students need to choose just **one** for this presentation.

Here are four examples of the message that they might choose for this presentation. They need to be able to say this message in one short sentence. A potential message might be:

Football is an exciting sport – and the World Cup is the most exciting.
Start playing football because it is more fun than some other more popular sports.
Go to a match – it is much more exciting than just watching it on television.
Women's football is becoming just as popular as the male version

Choosing the Approach

Once students have become aware of the purpose of their presentation and the message they want the audience to remember, it is time for them to choose an approach. The more original it is, the more interesting it will be to the audience and the more confidence they will have in delivering. Students may need some assistance in choosing an original, appropriate approach for their topic.

The Purpose

MAKE SURE YOU KNOW WHAT THE PURPOSE OF YOUR PRESENTATION IS

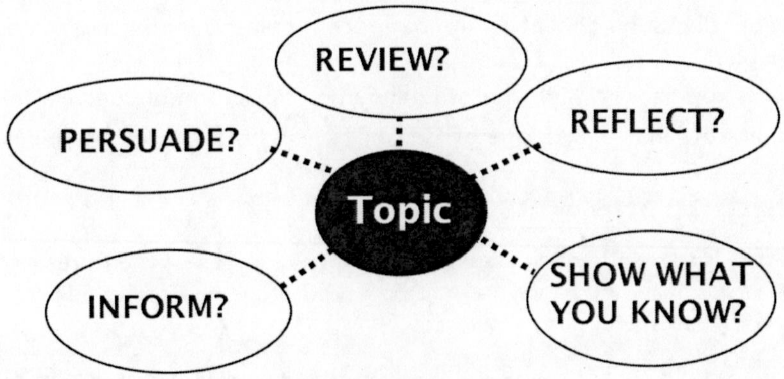

WHAT IS THE

ONE MESSAGE

YOU WANT THE AUDIENCE TO REMEMBER?

CHOOSING AN ORIGINAL APPROACH WILL MAKE IT MORE INTERESTING

DRAMATISATION	*DOCUMENTARY*
ROLE PLAY	*ALLEGORY*
HUMOUR	*SOME OTHER WAY*

Chapter 10

Speech Openings

Grab Their Attention

A speech is very much like a hit song on the radio - it has to have a 'hook' - something to grab the audience's attention in the first 30 or 40 seconds. This must be the main purpose of every opening - otherwise all the effort spent preparing could be wasted – because the audience won't be listening! The opening might also introduce some of the points of the presentation, but this must be secondary to gaining the audience's attention.

The ideal speech opening is like a well written newspaper article. The headline grabs your attention and the first few sentences tell you the main point of the article. There are some speakers who find this approach too 'up front'. They prefer to tantalise their audience, slowly revealing piece by piece, taking half the speech (or more) to make their message clear. While this approach *may* work with certain specialised subjects and certain audiences, generally it runs the risk of losing the audience's interest or of confusing them.

How long?

A good opening is sharp, snappy and to the point. The length of it should be between ten percent and twenty percent of the overall length of the speech. Ten percent should be the target but in short presentations (of only a few minutes) this may not be possible.

Some Techniques To Grab Attention

Any technique to get the audience's attention is valid - as long as it is relevant to the subject and doesn't offend anyone. Here are some that have proven to work well.

Shock them - by making a startling opening statement

The startling statement can be as shocking as the audience will allow - as long as it has some link (however small) with the subject.

Examples:

'*In the time I'll take to give this speech three football fields of rainforest will disappear!*' – a talk on saving the environment.

'*I'm an addict*' - a speech about the evils of fast food.

Some audience involvement could be added with this technique: Have one quarter of the audience stand and then say: '*Statistics show that this is how many people in this room will die of heart disease*'.

Arouse their Curiosity

This can best be done by appealing to that most basic of audience motivations '*What's in this for me?*' The speaker can 'whet their appetite' by a promise of valuable or interesting information to come.

Examples:

"I'm going to tell you how to make a million dollars in just ten years."

"By the time I finish, you will know all you need to know about the coolest Web sites!"

"Today I'm going to tell you about one of the world's greatest mysteries."

Ask a question

This technique virtually forces the audience to give you their attention - because a relevant question is going to have every person in the room trying to answer it in their own minds. Questions should be relatively simple and easy for them to answer. Asking a very complex, controversial question runs the risk of having audience members still thinking about their answer halfway through your speech. The purpose of the question is to get their full attention so they can then concentrate on what you have to say.

Examples

"*When was the last time you had a great thrill?*" (a speech promoting abseiling)

"*What sort of bike rider are you?*" (a speech on road safety)

"*How would you react if this happened to you ...?*"

Use visual aids and/or 'special effects'

Audio devices (e.g. sound effects) can give a very different, attention getting opening. Visual aids or effects can also work well (e.g. turning the lights out in a darkened room as a 'shock' opening for a speech on the dangers of underground mining).

Create a 'link' with the occasion

An interesting opening can be created by linking some aspect of the occasion to the topic of the presentation. This is especially effective if it has immediate relevance to a particular audience. For example:

The presentation might be on the anniversary of some occasion that can be linked to your topic. "*On this day twenty years ago, the first computer went on the market in Australia. Today, virtually every house has at least one of them.*"

The place the speech is to be presented might have some special significance. "*This is the building where all of our school's trophies are placed on show. On these walls you can see our greatest sporting achievements – and another great achievement is...*"

A recent news event might highlight an aspect of the topic. "*In today's newspaper there is a headline about a little old lady being bashed in the street. Another example of the subject of my talk today...bullying.*"

exercises

Ask students to use the five opening techniques for a speech topic that you provide. Suitable topics are:

Ageing in Our Society
Animal Rights
Global Warming
Self Image
Drugs in Our Society

Students choose one topic. This may be one of the above or a topic of an upcoming assignment. Using this one topic, they should write five opening lines; using one of the techniques in each. Allow them to be creative with facts and statistics; because they should not spend time researching. The aim of this exercise is to have them understand how they might use the techniques.

Shock them with a startling statement

Make them curious

Ask a question

Use visual aids and/or 'special effects'

Create a link

Speech Openings

THE MAIN PURPOSE OF AN OPENING IS:

GRAB THE AUDIENCE'S ATTENTION !

Ways to do this:

SHOCK THE AUDIENCE

Use a startling opening statement (facts, statistics, or your opinion)

Example: "*I was shocked when I found out how much...*"

MAKE THE AUDIENCE CURIOUS

Arouse their curiosity by telling them that it will be worth their while to listen.

Example: "*By the time I've finished today, you will know...*"

ASK A QUESTION

Audience members find it difficult to resist a question put to them. They feel they must answer it - and this ensures you have their attention.

Example: "*When was the last time you...*"

USE VISUAL AIDS OR SPECIAL EFFECTS

The visual component provides up to 55% of the message, so this is a logical way to have them take notice.

Examples: Show a graphic image. Change the lighting in the room.

CREATE A LINK

Linking your topic to some current event, the surroundings, etc gives it a special relevance - because it could only be said at this time.

Examples: "*On this day twenty years ago...*" "*The poster on our classroom wall is a constant reminder of...*"

Chapter 11

Memorable Conclusions

What the Audience Will Remember

Simply because it is the last thing that they will hear, an audience is likely to remember the conclusion more than any other part of the presentation. So, in order to make a conclusion work as effectively as possible, it is important that this part of the speech totally reinforces the 'main message' - that one main idea around which the entire presentation is written. The question to be asked is "*If this audience only remembers one thing from my presentation, what do I want it to be?*".

So often after a brilliantly original presentation which is packed with information, you will hear audience members saying to each other "*Well it certainly looked like a lot of work was put into that - but I wonder what the point of it all was*". This should never happen. The audience must be in no doubt as to what the main point is otherwise they will feel frustrated and won't remember anything.

How Long?

In general, the length of a conclusion should be about the same as that of an introduction (10-20% of the overall length).

The Summary

The conclusion is not the place to introduce new information. It should, instead, be a concise summary of the information in the body of the speech. If this information is complex, a list of the major points could be shown on a poster or projected image.

Link Back to the Opening

The most common cause of poor conclusions is failing to link back strongly enough to the opening. A conclusion should 'tie things up'; and the best way to do this is to refer back to the opening comments. If any promises were made as part of the introduction, make sure that they have been kept. For example, if in the opening it was said "*I'm going to show you how you can love using public transport*", this would need to be addressed in the conclusion. An example of this could be "*At the start of this presentation I promised I'd have you loving public transport. Now that you know how much you will save on car expenses, how much more convenient the new services are, and how much you'll be helping our city's environment, I'll bet you just can't wait to get out there and jump on a bus, train, tram or ferry!*"

If any startling or deliberately ambiguous statements or questions were made as part of the opening to get the audience's attention, ensure that these are cleared up. If this is not done, the audience members will feel frustrated - possibly even a little cheated. The ideal conclusion ties back neatly to the opening, which leaves the audience feeling satisfied and in no doubt as to what was the speaker's message.

The 'Call to Action'

If the presentation is attempting to have the audience members think differently about a particular matter, it is very effective if this is accompanied by a suggestion as to what they might be able to do to show they accept the speaker's point of view. For example, in a presentation about the environment, one simple suggestion on recycling could be included. In a report on a local annual festival, encourage everyone to mark the date in their diary for next year. The idea is to give the audience something simple and achievable to do to because the hope is they have accepted the message and they now want to do something about it.

'Sell' the Conclusion

The most common cause of an indifferent conclusion with students is that they fail to deliver it with sufficient confidence. It should be the most confident, 'upbeat' part of the presentation. Failings in this area are much more likely to occur in the vocal and visual delivery than the actual words.

Start at the End

Writing and preparing a speech in the order it will be delivered can often be a trap for students for a number of reasons:

- They create a good opening. Then they write the rest of the speech and struggle to link the conclusion strongly back to the opening.
- They can go into their presentation of the speech being much more familiar with the opening than the conclusion – making it extremely difficult to deliver the conclusion with the necessary confidence.

Students can avoid these traps by applying the following:

- Write the conclusion side-by-side with the opening. Some students find it easier to write the conclusion first – then make everything else in the speech lead up to this point.
- Practise the presentation in separate 'chunks' (opening, conclusion, sections of the body) and spend the most time on the conclusion. If a student is more familiar with the conclusion than the opening then, rather than working away from the part they know best as the speech progresses, they are actually working towards it.

exercise

To reinforce the message that the conclusion must link back to the opening – and that, often, the easiest way to achieve this is to create them side-by-side – take the openings the students wrote in the previous exercise and have students write a conclusion that links back to each opening.

Conclusions

The conclusion is important because the last thing that an audience hears may be the only thing that they remember.

It does not add any new information but it must -

- *summarise the content of the presentation*
- *restate the main message*

It links back to the opening so that the audience has a sense of completion - feeling that your presentation has come 'full circle'.

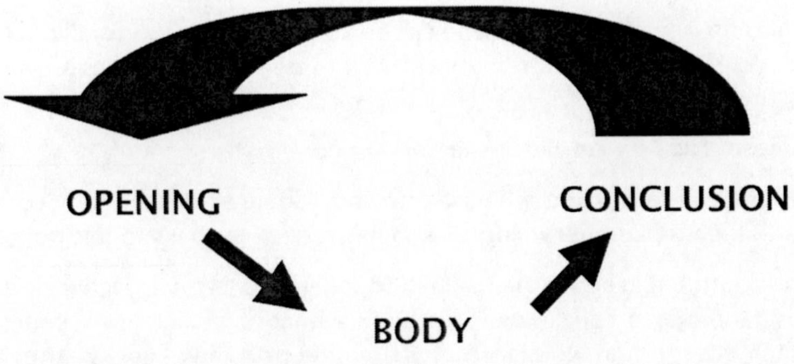

It will tie up any 'loose ends' - keeping any promises made as part of the opening or in the body of the presentation.

In a persuasive presentation you should always include something for the audience to do as part of the conclusion. What this says to them is

"If I have persuaded you in this presentation - here is what you can do about it."

It should be about the same length as the opening (10-20% of the overall length of the presentation).

DELIVER YOUR CONCLUSION WITH POWER!

Your conclusion should be delivered in a way that leaves your listeners in no doubt as to when you have finished your presentation. This means that the energy level of your presentation should rise to give a strong finish. Just as your opening needed to be forceful to get their attention, your conclusion has to be just as forceful to make them remember you.

Chapter 12

Writing to Speak

There are so many differences between the English used in a written presentation and a spoken one, it seems like they are separate languages. Some of the most obvious differences are listed here.

The Writer	The Speaker
If given the choice of using a short or long word will tend towards the longer one to enhance the presentation (and impress the reader/teacher) with the greatest possible use of vocabulary.	Will generally choose the shortest word that conveys the meaning. The role of spoken presentations is to communicate – not display the speaker's vocabulary. Shorter words are generally easier to say which means they are more likely to be delivered successfully.
Will try to avoid repetition.	Uses repetition for emphasis. While having the same word in consecutive sentences 'looks' wrong on the page; it has no such effect when spoken. Deliberate use of repetition in devices such as triplets (see next chapter) is one of the most common speech writing techniques.
Tends to write sentences that are long and can be quite complex. A good example is the use of adjectives (before and after the noun). Examples: *A big, strong man, John had no trouble lifting the box.* *Natalie, who always seemed to be able to say the right thing at the right time, was, on this occasion, lost for words.*	Keeps sentences as short as possible to make it easier for the audience to follow and easier to deliver. In the examples at left, a more logical structure or dividing it into two sentences will work much better when spoken. Examples: *John was a big, strong man - so he had no trouble lifting the box.* *Natalie always seemed to be able to say the right thing at the right time. But, on this occasion, even she was lost for words.*
Uses a language that tends to be more formal than conversational language.	Tries to keep the language as conversational as possible – although the tone may vary to suit the audience. One very obvious difference is the use of contractions – which are usually avoided when writing.
Is not generally concerned with the sound of the words.	Knows that the sound of a word is relevant. How easy a word is to pronounce may affect its choice.
Cannot generally refer to specific surroundings.	Can include references to the specific time, place and prevailing circumstances.

If we are reading and are confused by something the author has written, we have the ability to read the passage again and again till we do understand it. As an audience member we do not have that luxury. A speaker needs to remember that the listener only gets one chance to hear and understand what is said.

The best description of an effective speaking style is that of an enlarged conversation. It is important to give students permission and encouragement to use conversational – rather than formal – language. Otherwise, every presentation they deliver will sound like them reading aloud one of their written assignments.

exercises

Have students re-write the statements below in a style that will sound natural when spoken:

1. What I am about to say in my presentation is of great importance to every person present here today.
2. The principal, who saw that the students would not all fit into the bus, rang the company and demanded another vehicle.
3. Radiating a wonderful, sweet scent, the Pink Beauty rose is a favourite with florists.
4. There will be no variation to the price while the availability remains difficult.
5. Her manner indicated that she had received some very favourable news.

Writing to Speak

The rules for effective spoken English are different to the rules of written English. If you inappropriately apply the rules of written English you will create a presentation which is more difficult to deliver than it should be.

	When you write	When you speak
Formality	Tends to be formal	Informal - you need to sound conversational
Sentences & vocabulary	Can be complex	Shorter and simpler makes them easier to say.
Repetition	Avoided	Used regularly for reinforcement and clarity
Sounds of the words	Irrelevant	Important - always say a word/phrase aloud before choosing it.
References to recipients, surroundings, etc	Generally not possible	Use to increase relevance and immediacy

THE BEST STYLE FOR SPOKEN DELIVERY IS THAT OF AN ENLARGED CONVERSATION

Chapter 13

Devices for Speeches

Vivid words and picturesque language can bring a presentation alive. Incorporating some of the devices listed below will enhance any presentation.

Alliteration

An alliterative phrase (where two or more words in a phrase start with the same sound) gives the speaker something to really emphasise which makes that part of the presentation more memorable for the audience. For example: fear of failure, bad skin and a breaking voice, people power.

Catchphrases

A catchphrase is anything that 'catches' the attention and sticks in the memory. They are generally short, often humorous, and can significantly enhance the 'memorability' of a speech. They can come from anywhere - advertising slogans, bumper stickers, T-shirts. Catchphrases often use other devices such as alliteration, assonance and puns to enhance their 'catchiness'.

Examples:

- '*I have a dream*' (Martin Luther King)
- '*Just do it*' (Sporting brand slogan)

Juxtaposition

The dictionary meaning is to place one thing beside another. In speaking terms, this involves placing two opposites together to create a more dramatic impact. It is based on the principle that many things become clearer in contrast - just as black looks more dramatic against a white background and white looks 'whiter' against a black one. Some classic examples of juxtaposition have been used by Presidents of the USA:

John F Kennedy: '*Ask not what your country can do for you. Ask what you can do for your country.*'

Bill Clinton: - '*There is nothing that's wrong with America that can't be fixed by what's right with America.*'

Metaphors & Similes

Metaphors are based on describing one thing as something different, yet similar in one key aspect. For example, when an aggressive player is said to be a tiger, or when a classroom is said to be a torture chamber. Similes work on the same principle, except one thing is said to be 'like' something else. For example: "*Like lambs to the slaughter,our team ran onto the field.*"

Metaphors and similes are extremely effective in speeches. This is because they are so picturesque. An imaginative phrase can paint a very vivid picture in the mind of the audience member. Example: "*The decision hung above him like an angry storm cloud.*"

"*Public fraud is a cancer eating at the foundations of our society*"

Onomatopoeia

Onomatopoeia uses words which sound similar to the sounds they describe. Adding them to speeches can enliven them greatly through both greater imagery and more varied vocal usage. Good examples are words such as bang, hiss, crunch, rattle, buzz and splash.

Pun

The humorous use of a word in such a way as to suggest two or more meanings (Shorter Oxford Dictionary)

Although the traditional response to a pun from an audience is a groan - it's a groan with smiles on their faces. Be careful not to overuse it - once or twice in most speeches is adequate. e.g. "*I like all the forest animals, even leeches - I guess you could call me a bit of a sucker.*"

Rhyme

Rhyming words can add greatly to the 'catchiness'of a phrase. Used sparingly, rhyme makes a speech more memorable. Examples : "*Do the crime and do the time*" , "*drive to arrive alive*".

Signposts

It is very easy for an audience's attention to wander. Having regular 'signposts' that point the way or signal a change in direction to the audience help them to keep up. Some good examples –

In the opening: "*What I'm going to do today is cover three aspects of this very important subject*"

During the presentation: "*So, let's look at what we have covered so far.*"

In the conclusion: "*The most important point of all is...*"

"*If you only remember one thing, make sure it is this.*"

Obviously, the more complicated the presentation, the more 'signposts' are needed.

Triplets

In speaking, a certain amount of repetition adds impact and forcefulness to a presentation. Repetition is certainly used much more in writing a speech than it would be used in other writing.

A triplet is based on the principle that for some reason listeners find this repetition most effective in 'bunches' of three. If only two are used, a sufficient pattern of repetition is not established for it to have its effect. Somehow, four seems too many for most situations.

So, the idea of a triplet is to involve some degree of repetition. Triplets can come in a number of ways.

Firstly, they can be used to add more information. The phrase builds point by point, with the final (third) point as the main one:-

"*I was tired. I was cold. I was prepared to do anything to get a room for the night.*'

"*This practice is cruel, it's wasteful and, most of all, it's giving our children the wrong idea of what this world is about.*"

Other ways of using triplets are:

- repeating a word or phrase: *So much unemployment, so much despair, so much wasted opportunity.* OR *I was tired. I was cold. I was prepared to do anything to get a room for the night.*
- using three verbs: *it has been engineered for strength, designed for durability and built for the toughest conditions.*
- using three nouns: *every home needs one, every apartment needs one, every office building needs one.*

exercises

The following edited excerpt from "I Have A Dream" by Martin Luther King contains many examples of the devices mentioned in this chapter, particularly metaphors, alliteration, triplets and juxtaposition. Have students identify as many as possible.

> *Five score years ago, a great American, in whose symbolic shadow we stand, signed the Emancipation Proclamation. This momentous decree came as a great beacon light of hope to millions of Negro slaves who had been seared in the flames of withering injustice. It came as a joyous daybreak to end the long night of captivity.*
>
> *But one hundred years later, we must face the tragic fact that the Negro is still not free. One hundred years later, the life of the Negro is still sadly crippled by the manacles of segregation and the chains of discrimination. One hundred years later, the Negro lives on a lonely island of poverty in the midst of a vast ocean of material prosperity.*
>
> *Now is the time to rise from the dark and desolate valley of segregation to the sunlit path of racial justice.*
>
> *Now is the time to open the doors of opportunity to all of God's children.*
>
> *Now is the time to lift our nation from the quick sands of racial injustice to the solid rock of brotherhood.*
>
> *It would be fatal for the nation to overlook the urgency of the moment and to underestimate the determination of the Negro. This sweltering summer of the Negro's legitimate discontent will not pass until there is an invigorating autumn of freedom and equality. Nineteen sixty-three is not an end, but a beginning.*
>
> *This is our hope. This is the faith with which I return to the South. With this faith we will be able to hew out of the mountain of despair a stone of hope. With this faith we will be able to transform the jangling discords of our nation into a beautiful symphony of brotherhood. With this faith we will be able to work together, to pray together, to struggle together, to go to jail together, to stand up for freedom together, knowing that we will be free one day.*

Devices for Speeches

Alliteration

is created when two or more words in phrase start with the same sound. It has the effect of making a phrase more memorable. For example: ***f***ear of ***f***ailure, ***p***eople ***p***ower.

A **Catchphrase**

'catches' the attention and sticks in the memory. They are generally short, often humorous and can make your speech more memorable. For example: *Oh what a feeling* OR *Just do it.*

Juxtaposition

places two opposites together to create a more dramatic impact. It works on the idea that many things become clearer in contrast. For example: *"Ask not what your country can do for you. Ask what you can do for your country."* OR *"It's nice to be important, but it's more important to be nice."*

A **Metaphor**

makes a comparison between two things, identifying one with the other. For example: a classroom is said to be a *torture chamber*. Public fraud is a *cancer – eating at the foundations of our society.*

Onomatopoeia

is the use of words that sound similar to the sounds they describe. For example: *crunch, rattle, hiss* and *splash.*

Pun.

This device uses words in a humorous way that suggests two or more meanings. For example: *"He wanted desperately to be a good golfer – you could say he had a driving ambition."*

Rhyming words

can add greatly to the 'catchiness' of a phrase. Used sparingly, rhyme makes a speech more memorable. Examples : "Do the crime and do the time" , "drive to arrive alive".

Signposts

help keep an audience on track. Regular signposts point the way or signal a new idea to your audience. For example:

In the opening: *"What I'm going to do today is cover three aspects of this very important subject"*

During the presentation: *"So, let's look at what we have covered so far."*

In the conclusion: *"The most important point of all is..."*

"If you only remember one thing, make sure it is this."

Obviously, the more complicated your presentation, the more 'signposts' you will need.

Similes

are really useful for graphic description - so they serve the same purpose as metaphors. Similes are distinguished by their use of the word 'like'. For example: He came running across the park *like an excited puppy.*

A **Triplet**

adds impact by use of repetition in 'bunches' of three. Triplets can be used in a number of ways. For example:

- repeating a word/phrase: *So much unemployment, so much despair, so much wasted opportunity.* OR *I was tired. I was cold. I was prepared to do anything to get a room for the night.*
- using three verbs: *it has been engineered for strength, designed for durability and built for the toughest conditions.*
- using three nouns: *every home needs one, every apartment needs one, every office building needs one.*

Chapter 14

Story Telling

Purpose

The informality of telling a story helps your students to become less fearful in a speaking situation. Telling stories is a skill they already possess – albeit in different circumstances.

The advantages of stories in speeches are:

1. Audiences like stories – the narrative engages them.
2. The story is the part of a speech where the speaker is least likely to lose their way.
3. The story is often the part of a presentation that they are most likely to remember.

Preparation

Ensure your students select a story that is appropriate for retelling. It needs to have a clear plot, an interesting beginning, logical development of key ideas, some conflict and a satisfying conclusion. They do not have to remember the words of the writer. Indeed they use their own with perhaps a few well chosen phrases from the actual story.

Have students read the story a couple of times. The first time is for enjoyment and then the next time is to visualise each scene. Your students need to be encouraged to sense the emotions of the situation.

The mind of an audience member can be thought of as a blank canvas - to which a speaker adds form, colour and action with the right words. The more clearly and vividly that picture is painted the more effective (and memorable) a speech will be.

The basic principle of describing any scene is to make it easy for the audience to follow. Starting with the background and working forward is logical and allows people to build up the scene for themselves bit-by-bit. The most common mistake made by speakers in this area is to start describing the action before the background has been fully established. This will confuse the audience members as the speaker tries to 'fill in' necessary bits of the background while telling the story.

Painting word pictures is like composing a landscape:

- 'draw' in the background – set the scene
- introduce the characters
- describe the action

Describing People

Here are some points which will help with descriptions of people.

- Use the 'Two Word Generalisation'.

  By using a noun that describes a generalised grouping of people and an appropriate descriptive adjective, most descriptions of people can be achieved quite vividly in the audience's minds.

  For example, if someone is described as a kindly grandmother, everyone in the audience will immediately imagine someone - their own grandmother, someone else's grandmother, a character from TV. It doesn't really matter that each person might be imagining a different 'kindly grandmother'. What does matter is that each person will have a clear picture in their mind that the speaker can then manipulate into a story.

- Give their general age.

  Giving a general age range seems to be one of the quickest ways to describe people. Often, the descriptive noun (see 'Generalised Groupings" above) will achieve this (a teenager, a baby boomer, etc.).

- Give your characters names.

  A name makes a character come alive. Audience members find it easier to relate to and remember characters with a name. It also makes description of any story easier and more concise as you are not stuck with clumsy descriptions like "*the first person said to the second person...*".

Dialogue

One way to bring a story alive is with use of dialogue. Try to have students replace bland paraphrasing of the conversation with the actual words.

For example:

replace: *And then Indira suggested that we all go down to the park which she said would be fun.*

with: *Then Indira said, "Let's go down to the park. It'll be fun!"*

This changes the sentence into a passage that will sound more interesting because it gives more opportunity for vocal variety.

The Lesson Learned

A good story has a message. This message should reflect the message of the speech. Finishing the story with a 'message statement' ensures it reinforces the message in the most powerful way.

exercises

1. For this exercise you will need landscape images (magazines such as Australian Geographic or National Geographic are excellent for this) – one for each student.

   Have students work in pairs. One student chooses a picture of a scene. **The other student must not see the image.** In the space of one minute, the student with the image describes the scene to the partner as fully as possible. At the end of the one minute, they show the scene to their partner and receive feedback about the accuracy of their description.

   Repeat the exercise – switching roles.

   Remind students about the principle of describing the scene from the back and moving forward.

2. Have students write a description of the scene above in less than eighty words - starting with the background and working forward. (That is: describe the sky and white mountains first and the woman last.) This should be written for it to be spoken, so pay particular attention to the sounds of the words and the images that they convey.

3. Have students write a story about your first day at school. Have them describe the story by following these steps:

   - **Set the Scene**

     What day of the week was it?

     What was the weather like?

     How old were you?

     How did you get to school?

     Which entrance did you arrive at?

     What did it look like when you arrived?

     How did you feel about going to a new school?

   - **Introduce the characters**

     Who was the first person you saw when you arrived?

     Who was the first student that spoke to you?

     Was there anybody that you already knew?

     Who was the first teacher who spoke to you?

     Who was the one person you remember most from your first day?

   - **Describe the dialogue**

     Choose one person you described in the section above and tell about a conversation you had with them. It doesn't matter if you can't remember exactly what was said. Describe the conversation in dialogue, that is: I said "...", then he said "..."

Story Telling

Why stories work so well in speeches:

Audiences love stories -	so you know you're giving them what they want.
Audiences remember stories -	so you can make your speech more memorable
Stories are easy to remember -	it's unlikely for you to go blank telling a story.

Build up the story in their minds:

Set the scene

Introduce the characters

Describe the action & dialogue

Chapter 15

The Vocal Message

The way the voice is used can contribute five times as much to the message as the actual words. The way a speaker vocalises the words in a speech should never be accidental.

Volume

Being an 'enlarged conversation', the effective volume for a presentation may feel a little too loud to the speaker. Not being able to hear a speaker annoys audiences intensely

Tone

Tone of voice carries emotion and engagement. The alternative is monotone – which is what some speakers achieve when they read their notes &/or slides.

Rate

An average of 135words/minute is achieved with some passages at 160 wpm and others (the key points) at 60 wpm. Choosing which passages should be faster or slower increases the audience's understanding. (Faster for describing context, slower for key points.)

Inflection

Nervousness often causes speakers to finish phrases with a rising inflection – making them sound uncertain or pleading. Using a falling inflection will turn a phrase into a statement of authority.

Emphasis

The word that is emphasised affects the meaning of the phrase/sentence.

Emphasise key words and numbers – the right amount may feel 'too big' at first

Pause

Audiences love pauses. They give them a chance to catch up &/or absorb the message. Pauses need to be 2-3 sec (in real time) to work effectively.

Here are just a few examples of how a speaker might make the best use of the vocal component:

- deliberately slowing down and emphasising key words in the sentence that carries the main message.
- increasing the pace of delivery in an action narrative.
- lowering the volume and softening the tone in a sad passage.
- having the voice deliberately drop towards the end of a sentence where the speaker wants to sound authoritative.
- following a thought-provoking statement with a longer than average pause.

exercises

1. In pairs, tell each other your first name (as if they do not already know it). In turn, say the other person's name to them in the following ways

   Formally

   Friendly

   Irritated (eg they are making you late for an appointment)

   Angry (eg they made you miss the appointment)

   Cajoling (eg you want them to do you a favour)

   Identify the differences in tone and inflection that allowed you to express such a wide range of meaning with just the one word.

2. Say the sentence "This is really important" in the following ways -

   With your voice tone rising on the word 'important'

   With your voice tone falling on the word 'important'

   Notice the difference in meaning. Which sounds more confident?

   Use different pitch and tone of voice to give the following words different meanings –

   Fantastic!

   That's very smart!

3. Examine the following passage from AB (Banjo) Patterson's *The Man from Snowy River* to determine how variation in pace and volume could make the delivery more effective.

   - Identify two lines that you would speak more quickly and explain why.
   - Identify a line that you would speak more slowly and explain why.
   - Identify two lines that you would speak more loudly and explain why.

   When they reached the mountain's summit, even Clancy took a pull,
   It well might make the boldest hold their breath
   The wild hop scrub grew thickly, and the hidden ground was full
   Of wombat holes, and any slip was death.
   But the man from Snowy River let the pony have his head,
   And he swung his stockwhip round and gave a cheer,
   And he raced him down the mountain like a torrent down its bed,
   While the others stood and watched in very fear.
   He sent the flintstones flying, but the pony kept his feet,
   He cleared the fallen timber in his stride,
   And the man from Snowy River never shifted in his seat -
   It was grand to see that mountain horseman ride.
   Through the stringybarks and saplings, on the rough and broken ground,
   Down the hillside at a racing pace he went;
   And he never drew the bridle till he landed safe and sound,
   At the bottom of that terrible descent.

The Vocal Message

When you are giving a speech, people will listen more if it sounds interesting.

You make your voice sound interesting with...

Volume

Make sure you're loud enough so that everybody can hear you.

Pace

Aim for an average of 130-150 words per minute; but, most importantly, have some parts that are FASTER and some that are SLOWER. This is what makes it interesting.

Tone

Tone of voice shows feelings. Varying your tone to suit the different parts of the speech adds interest. Don't do this and you risk the dreaded MONOTONE.

Pause

The most effective use of voice is sometimes when you don't use it. Choose the places in your presentation where you really want your point to 'sink in' and plan to pause (stop speaking for 3 seconds)

Articulation

Make sure you say every word clearly so that everybody can understand you.

Preparing for a speech means saying it ALOUD.

Chapter 16

The Visual Message

Even though it contributes more to the message than the other two components (verbal and vocal) combined, the visual component is often overlooked in preparation. These are the aspects that students should consider as part of the speech writing process.

Body Language

The visual part of a speech relates very much to 'body language'. An audience starts making judgements about a speaker the moment the presentation starts. Nervous fidgets, the placing of hands in pockets or behind the back, touching of hair all give signs that are negative or distracting and should be eliminated in presentations.

'Speaker Neutral' Stance

The most natural stance is to have the arms by the side in a relaxed manner, feet about the same distance apart as shoulder-width, with weight evenly balanced on both feet. Feeling natural in this 'speaker neutral' stance is one of the hardest things in public speaking; but the earlier a person becomes accustomed to this, the faster they will progress in speaking confidence. Most importantly, it stops bad habits starting that are so hard to break later on.

'Writing' Gestures

Gestures are an integral part of any speech. As such, they require some thought as to their appropriateness and effectiveness. Hand and arm gestures that 'open up' the body (ie arms open, palms up) are the most effective. Using appropriate gestures is a matter of considering the words and ideas in a speech and devising the best one for the circumstances. Some examples will serve to illustrate; size can be shown by use of arms, numbers by the use of fingers, body movement by use of posture.

Gestures should not happen by accident. They need as much planning as the words. It is not essential, or even desirable, to 'write' every gesture in a presentation. But, if a speaker plans to include and practise gestures for key moments in a speech it will -

- Add impact to the parts of that speech that are most important.
- Eliminate repetitive gestures. All speakers have certain idiosyncratic gestures and these can become repetitive if not consciously replaced with something. That is, it is extremely difficult to eliminate a 'negative' unless you have a 'positive' to replace it.

The Eyes Have It

Without doubt, the part of body language that contributes most to a speaker's credibility is eye contact. Ironically, this is the one thing which cannot be rehearsed. Here are some helpful hints:

Dwell - don't scan

Eye contact means what it says - making contact. That means looking at someone long enough to meet their eyes - so that for those few seconds the speaker is talking **just to** that person. Scanning, where the speaker looks across a line of eyes (but never really makes contact) should be avoided.

Eye contact with the page doesn't count

A speaker should try to look at the audience whenever saying anything. This may mean that the delivery will be a little slower as the speaker looks down, reads the notes then looks up to say it. However, the advantages will be seen in the way the presentation is received with greater interest by the audience. People become quickly bored if they are just read to. Effective speech notes are essential for good eye contact.

First find a friendly face

It helps if a speaker can choose who they will look at for the early part of their presentation. This eliminates one 'risk factor' at the start and so can be a good confidence builder. Students may choose to make eye contact with just two or three people for the first 30 seconds of their presentation – in 3-5 second 'bursts'. This might be three friends (as long as they are confident these friends won't use the occasion for any practical jokes). They might even choose you; which could help them overcome initial nervousness. For this reason, it can be a good idea – as long as they don't spend the entire presentation talking to you.

Visual Aids

Use of visual aids requires careful planning, because what can add greatly to a presentation can also distract from it.

There are three basic rules in the creation of images for audiences -

1. Keep it short, simple, clear & LARGE. A good rule of thumb is 'it should be the same as you'd use on the front of a t-shirt'. If using a word processor, 24 point should be the smallest you use.
2. Aim for the highest possible contrast between the lettering or graphic and the background. Often what looks great on a computer screen will look washed out or illegible when projected in a half darkened room.
3. The relevant visual should ONLY be able to be seen by the audience while the speaker is talking about that point. With videos and computer generated images (eg PowerPoint®), particular care is required because a hissing 'snowy' screen or blinking cursor is just as distracting. Make sure you know how to blank the screen when required.

Warning: While visual aids can add to a presentation, they can also be a great distraction – taking away preparation time that should be spent on practising vocal delivery and body language.

exercises

1. Have students think of and demonstrate a gesture (facial expression + hand/arm/ body movements) to go with the following words:

huge	*sick*
tiny	*busy*
boring	*relaxed*
scary	*excited*
happy	*sad*

2. Have students think of and demonstrate a series of gestures to accompany the following phrases:

   "I opened the cupboard to find it empty!"

   "This is really important"

   "I was so confused – I didn't know which way was up and which was down"

   "I could reach it, but only if I got up on the tips of my toes"

   "The only way we could get out was to squeeze through this really tiny hole near the floor."

3. Have students devise a PowerPoint® slide to show that in every speech –

   7% of the message comes from the words

   38% of the message comes from the voice

   55% of the message comes from what they see

Body Language

The Visual part of a speech (ie. what an audience sees) is very important - making up over half of the message we give out.

Speaker Neutral Stance

- Arms relaxed by your side.
- Feet are shoulder-distance apart with weight evenly balanced on each foot.
- Adopt the 'speaker neutral stance' to start and make your gestures from this position.

Gestures are an important part of any speech.

- Gestures need as much planning as words. They add impact to the parts of your speech you want your audience to remember.

  Examples

  size can be shown by use of your hands and arms

  numbers by use of fingers

  Think of one or two gestures you can use in your presentation and practise them.

The Eyes

- The part of body language that is most important is eye contact,
- Eye contact means looking at someone long enough for them to meet your eyes.
- Try to look at the audience as you are speaking, even if it means a slower delivery. Look down, read the notes /passage then look up and say it.
- ALWAYS look at your audience whenever you say ANYTHING.

Don't...

- Put your hands in your pockets, behind your back or clasped in front
- Fold your arms or put your hands on your hips
- Shuffle your feet
- Fiddle with your clothes
- Read from your notes
- Look at the floor or ceiling (unless it's a deliberate gesture)

Using Projected Images (eg PowerPoint®)

- LARGE print
- High contrast (between words and background)
- Only relevant words and images shown (grey out other text or blank screen)

Chapter 17

The Seminar or Group Style Presentation

In a seminar style presentation, a variety of methods is available to put the message across.

Lecture :

allows the speaker to control the process but requires special effort to maintain audience attention as there is no involvement from them.

Question and Answer :

can energise the audience but gives up some control.

Case Studies:

allows audience to consider real-life situations and offer solutions.

Experiential Activities:

allows audience to be actively involved. Breaks the ice and adds life to the presentation.

Demonstrations:

allows the presenter to show a correct behaviour, technique or process.

Media Activities:

use charts, slides, videos.

Role Playing:

allows the presenter to select a problem, create a plot and characters and finally lead the group to a discussion and solution of the problem.

A seminar is often given in a group situation. Here are some guidelines for when you are required to prepare and present in a group.

Guidelines for Segments of Less than Ten Minutes

There is not really much time to do anything other than deliver a presentation (with, perhaps, a little audience involvement). Try to add variety with:

- Some small audience activity (eg having all close their eyes for a few seconds in a presentation on "Inside a Black Hole").
- Some short audio or visual input, for example a short sound or video recording, an OHP of a relevant graph or a number of "samples" for distribution to the audience (being careful to make sure it supports the presentation, rather than overwhelms or replaces it).

When there is more than one person involved in the presentation there is automatically available a much larger range of possibilities in the style of the presentation and the opportunities for originality. Some examples of this are-

- Role Play (to show different ways of handling a problem)
- Interview (for example TV current affairs show)
- Re-enactment of an important event in history

Guidelines for 10-20 Minute Segments

This length of time is too short for a real workshop but still leaves scope for considerable audience interaction.

Generally what works best is a combination of 50% presentation and 50% group discussion or activity.

This discussion/activity has to be carefully governed otherwise time will over-run.

With regard to audience questions, the two choices are:

1. To invite questions throughout (has the advantage of immediacy, but can be disruptive to the flow)
2. To have a specific Question & Answer (Q&A) time at the end. This is easier to control and often more efficient as many questions are answered in the body of the segment. The danger is that the Q&A session will become focused on an issue other than the main one, leaving the audience confused as to what the message really is. If there is a Q&A session at the end of the presentation, there needs to be a strong final 'wrapping up' statement to conclude it.

Above all, the speaker must remain in control whilst allowing all audience members to feel that they can participate.

The discussion/activity should be structured very carefully. What is possible is determined by the size of the group. With only 15-20 minutes there will not be time to achieve a great deal - but there still should be something to add some variety to the presentation.

Possible formats

(working on an overall time of 20 minutes)

Format A	Formal "lecture style" presentation	10 mins
	Formal Q&A session	10 min
Format B	"Tutorial style" presentation	
	(where the presenters invite questions throughout the presentation)	20min
Format C	Information (content) delivery	5 min
	Discussion (in large group or pairs/small group)*	10 min
	Q&A	5 min

*A large group discussion involves all the people in the room with audience members contributing their ideas one at a time as designated by a 'controller' at the front of the room. Pairs or small group (3-6) work involves a presenter setting a discussion topic or problem for the audience members to discuss in pairs or small groups. If appropriate and there is sufficient time, ask a representative of each small group to share the results of their discussion with everyone. However, if there is a set Q&A time, this would probably be unnecessary.

These are only meant as a few prompters to help presenters to develop their own formats.

Remember -

1. Time every segment
2. Always plan for shorter than allowed, ie for 15 min. plan 13 min., for 20 min plan 18 min.

Guidelines for Segments of 30 Minutes or More

Any time allowance of 30+ minutes allows time for workshops, discussion groups and role plays.

Unless otherwise directed, aim for an information to activity ratio of between one-third and one-half (ie in a 30 minute segment, information delivery should be between 10 and 15 minutes).

Some suggestions which have worked well for session presenters in the past are:

- Present a problem scenario for small groups (2-6) to solve followed by one member of each small group telling everyone their solution.
- Involve all in a group activity then conduct a large group discussion on the lessons learned in the activity and how these can be applied.
- Present information followed by small group work to discuss implementation strategies then a large group debrief to share information and discuss it. A suggested schedule for a 40 minute session like this would be:

Information presentation	15min
Small group work	10min
Large group work	10min
Closing summary	5 min
	40min

Guidelines for working in groups

The most common problem when trying to organise group work is in 'task definition' - simply having everyone understand what it is that is required of them. Often it can help to choose a 'sample' group from the audience and have them demonstrate the exercise for everyone else.

Often, particularly with the longer sessions, there will be a requirement to present as a group. This offers great possibilities in originality of presentation but requires more preparation and rehearsal. Often a brilliantly conceived presentation has failed to impress on the day through lack of preparation whilst a group of otherwise less confident presenters has looked very self assured - simply because they had taken the time to prepare properly.

A well prepared group presentation runs like a well directed play. Every participant knows exactly what they should be doing and where they should be standing at any given second. One presenter "backs up" the other, for example, stepping in to switch on an OHP, giving the presentation an air of professionalism that makes it stand out from the rest.

When a group mark is to be awarded, it is important to ensure that each member of the group receives roughly the same time in front of the audience. Allowing the one confident member of your group to do all the talking will result in the group mark being much lower than if all members had contributed equally. Sometimes in their keenness to give each member equal time some groups compromise the originality of their presentation by choosing predictable formats. For example, here are two options for a thirty minute presentation by a group of three -

PREDICTABLE		**ORIGINAL**	
Presenter A:	10min	Presenter A:	2min
Presenter B:	10min	Presenter B:	5min
Presenter C:	10min	Presenters A&C :	15min
		Presenter B:	8min

Group presentations show the ability of the members to prepare and present as a team. To be successful, all the team members should have the same vision of what they want to achieve – and what is required of each person to achieve this. This will show through in the quality, cohesion and, hopefully, the assessment of the final presentation.

Chapter 18

Speech Notes

The right notes help a speaker to focus on what they're saying at the time and not have to worry about what they'll say next. The trouble is that the type of notes chosen and the way that they're prepared by most speakers act as a hindrance. The options available are listed below -

A Full Text

Should only be used is there is a specific requirement to read specific passages.

- Makes the speaker read (destroying the all important eye contact).
- Turns the voice into a monotone.
- Means the speaker is obligated to stay near the lectern (or whatever holds the notes)
- Makes it very easy to lose one's place (meaning speakers are more likely to keep their eyes 'glued' to the page)

If a full script **must** be used the following points will help -

- Type it double-spaced with each sentence starting a new line. Never carry a sentence from one page to another.
- Only use one side of the page and use separate pages (not joined together in a pad).
- Number the pages and hold with a paper clip if necessary but DO NOT STAPLE
- When you are about to speak, place all pages to one side of the lectern and slide the pages across as you've finished with them. This avoids any turning of pages which is obvious to the audience.

Use every method possible (underlining, highlighting, bolding, etc.) to make it easier to find the right place again after looking up.

Prompt Notes

These are a much better option -

- Allow more eye contact (pauses to look down can be natural).
- Don't tie the speaker to the lectern so much.
- Can be as brief as the speaker's knowledge of the topic will let them be. In most cases, two A4 pages will hold ample prompt notes for a detailed presentation. This means they can be put down and never need to be touched during the presentation.
- Notes do not have to be restricted to words – many people find that symbols, signs and drawings work better for them. 'Mind Maps' work well for many people.

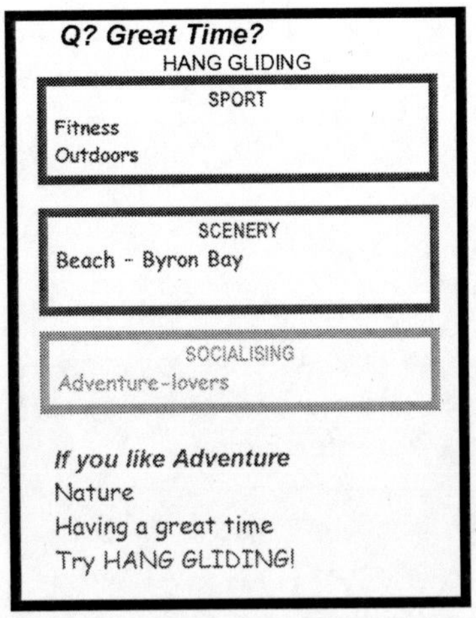

Uses colour and boxes to make information easier to find quickly.

Uses images which often prompt the memory faster.

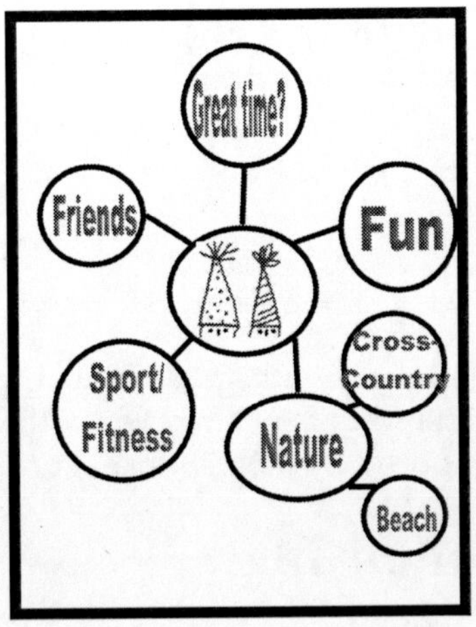

Uses a 'mind map' to connect the topics of the presentation.

exercises

Have students think of a story they could tell about a favourite holiday spot. This story should include a description of the place and why it is so favoured. If delivered as a speech, it would take less than five minutes.

Using this content, have them create speech notes using the three methods described here:

- colour and boxes
- images
- mind Maps

Speech Notes

A Full Text

Should only be used is there is a specific requirement to read. It:

- Turns your voice into a monotone.
- Makes it very easy to lose your place

If a full script **must** be used the following points will help -

- Type it double-spaced with each sentence starting a new line. Never carry a sentence from one page to another.
- Only use one side of the page and use separate pages (not joined together in a pad).
- Use every method possible (underlining, highlighting, bolding, etc.) to make it easier to find the right place again after looking up.

Prompt Notes

These are a much better option -

- Allow more eye contact (pauses to look down can be natural).
- Can be very brief - yet very effective.
- Notes do not have to be restricted to words - many people find that symbols, signs and drawings work better for them. 'Mind Maps' work well for many people.

Uses colour and boxes to make information easier to find quickly.

Uses images which often prompt the memory faster.

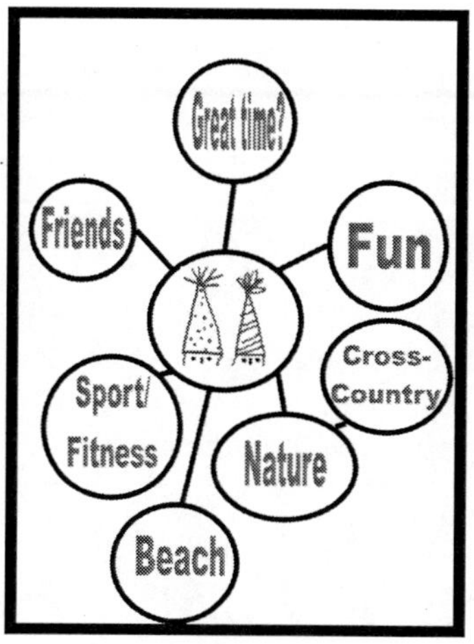

Uses a 'mind map' to connect the topics of the presentation.

Chapter 19

Impromptu Speaking

Be Prepared

There is a common misconception that you cannot be prepared for speaking impromptu. While you obviously cannot predict what a topic might be, there are ways to be able to speak 'off the cuff' with confidence on any occasion.

One of the greatest fears in impromptu speaking is that of going 'blank'. If, however, one works to a pre-defined plan, this fear is minimised. Speakers will discover that they have something to say on almost any subject – if they can find some way of getting past the panic that naturally occurs when we are asked to speak unexpectedly. Everyone has had the experience of thinking of the perfect response – twenty minutes later! Experienced speakers have found that using impromptu plans helps them to come up with the right response at the right time.

PRES

One of the most versatile plans is called PRES. This stands for –

POINT

REASON

EXAMPLE

SUMMARY

1. .Some people find that having 'lead in' phrases helps them to use the plan.
2. Make a **point** with a confident opening line such as "*I believe that...*" or "*I think we should...*".
3. State the **reason** with a line such as "*This is because...*" or "*The reason I say this is...*".
4. Give an **example** in the form of a story. A good lead in phrase might be "*Why, just the other day...*"

   or "*A good example of this was reported in the paper only recently.*"
5. Include a **summary** of your point. This reinforces your opening and gives a very clear and confident conclusion. You could start with "*And so you'll see, that's why I said...*"

By following this plan the speaker automatically has a 'prompt' as to what to say next. It gives the overall 'mini speech' an opening, body and conclusion as well as an air of confidence. It encourages the speaker to tell a story and linking a point to a story has proven to be one of the most effective ways of making the point more memorable. It also has the advantage of being very popular with audiences!

Best of all, PRES works *every* time, in *any* situation.

Using PRES for Prepared Speeches

PRES is also excellent as a plan for when a speaker <u>does</u> have time to prepare in advance.

It can be adapted for longer, more complex presentations by simply extending the 'middle' so that, in effect it becomes PRERES. There may be two or three reasons to back up the main point. Each reason is accompanied by an example.

The Past, Present, Future Plan

Another plan that is not quite as versatile as PRES, but can still be very useful is known as Past, Present, Future. This three-step plan has the speaker talking about what the subject was like years ago, the situation now and some speculation as to what it might be like in the future. This approach can also be made easier by the use of prompt phrases.

The speaker could open with	*"In the past..."*
Then follow this with	*"Today the situation is very different..."*
And conclude with	*"In the future, I believe we will see..."*

exercises

In pairs, practice using each of the three plans. For each exercise, use the Plan designated. Stand facing each other and take turns at speaking on a topic that is given 'on the spot'. Ensure that the person speaking is able to see a copy of the Plan being used. The topic may be given individually by the non speaking partner, or a topic may be given to the whole group. Aim to speak for at least one minute. The non speaking partner should give a sign when the minute is almost expired to allow the speaker to start their conclusion (if they haven't already).

1 **Past, Present, Future**

Simple topics such as motor vehicles, computers, houses, etc are suggested.

2 **PRES**

Suggested topics are any that require the speaker to take a point of view; eg the environment, the pursuit of wealth, violence in sport.

what you need to know about...

Impromptu Speaking

The PRES Plan

POINT
REASON
EXAMPLE
SUMMARY

STEP 1 Make a **point** with a confident opening line such as "*I believe that...*" or "*I think we should...*".

STEP 2 State the **reason** starting with words such as "*This is because...*" or "*The reason I say this is...*".

STEP 3 Give an **example** in the form of a story. A good lead in phrase might be "*Why, just the other day...*" or "*A good example of this was reported in the paper only recently.*"

STEP 4 Include a **summary** of your point. This reinforces your opening and gives a very clear and confident conclusion. You could start with "*And so you'll see, that's why I said...*"

The Past - Present - Future Plan

This three-step plan has the speaker talking about what the subject was like years ago, the situation now and some speculation as to what it might be like in the future.

STEP 1 "*In the past...*"
STEP 2 "*Today the situation is very different...*"
STEP 3 "*In the future, I believe we will see...*"

Chapter 20

Oral Interpretation & Reading Aloud

Purpose

At the outset, students need to understand that the skill of reading aloud is worth developing. Have them consider the various ways in which they see this skill used.

Throughout life, they may be called upon to read a report to a board, to read out minutes from a meeting, to read at a church service or to read to their children. Regardless of the ubiquity of multi-media, there are still many situations that require good clear reading that reinforces the beauty of the words or the importance of the message.

Definition

Oral interpretation can be defined as reading aloud from the written word to allow meaning to be conveyed to listeners. In effect, you are the link between author and audience. The purpose may be to inform to persuade, to entertain, to motivate or to encourage action.

Requirements

Successful oral reading requires that the speaker knows the material so well that its meanings, ideas, and nuances are clearly interpreted. Speakers should know the material well enough to be able to answer the following questions:

- Who is speaking? The author or main character or someone outside the story.
- Who is the listener? Is it slanted towards particular audience? Is the person speaking to his mother, his brother, a friend?
- When and where does the selection take place?
- What is the plot? What happens?
- When does the climax occur?
- What is the primary mood?
- Is there a theme?

Selecting an Oral Reading

The selection of the reading should be guided by these criteria:

- Suitability for the speaker. Students are best advised to keep to passages that they are able to interpret and read confidently. A piece that involves multiple characters is best left for only the most experienced speakers.
- Suitability for the audience. Audience analysis will help avoid anything inappropriate.
- Matching the occasion. A formal occasion may require different subject matter and/or from one that is less formal.
- Consideration of the venue. The size of the room and the seating arrangements could be factors in selecting a piece. A moving and emotional piece may not work well in a large and impersonal hall.

Delivery

Even though this is a reading, the same combination of verbal/vocal/visual communication is at work. Effective oral interpretation requires much more than just getting the words right. The vocal delivery should bring the reading alive. The speaker's facial expression will, ideally, match the tone of the reading; and regular eye contact will ensure that a connection with the audience is maintained.

HINT: A speaker should practise looking up at the end of every sentence. Then, when they are confident about finding their place when they look down again, they can start looking up as they say the last few words of each sentence. Gradually, they can extend this to where they are making eye contact for about half the time they are speaking.

Preparation

To prepare correctly, a speaker should:

- ensure that they understand the meaning of every word in the passage
- check for all punctuation - as this can change meaning dramatically
- research the circumstances surrounding the writing of the piece
- read aloud – practicing variation in pace, pauses and emphasis
- practise reading and looking up regularly to allow more eye contact with the audience.

HINT: If it's allowable, it can be helpful to underline words you want to emphasise and use forward slashes to indicate pauses: / for a short pause, // for a longer one.

exercises

Lead your students gently into this speaking style by trying some easier and interesting examples.

- Go to the Horoscopes in any magazine or paper and have students read their own horoscope to the audience.
- Select a children's book that requires good reading skills to fully appreciate the material.
- Select an article from a teenage magazine that has a simple message.
- Choose a selection of suitable poems from an anthology.
- Choose a selection from one of the many books of short inspirational sayings that are widely published.
- Choose a selection of Short Stories that are appropriate to your class.

ORAL INTERPRETATION AND READING ALOUD

Preparation

Your Choice – be sure it's

- Suitable for you. A piece that involves multiple characters is best left for only the most experienced speakers.
- Suitable for your audience.
- Matching the occasion.

Your Reading – what you should understand about it...

- Who is speaking? Is it the author? Is it the main character? Someone else?
- Who is the listener? Is it slanted towards particular audience? Is the author speaking to a relative, a friend?
- When and where does the selection take place?
- What is the plot? What happens?
- When does the climax occur?
- What is the primary mood?
- Is there a theme?

What you should know about it..

- Ensure that you understand the meaning of every word in the passage.
- Check for all punctuation - as this can change meaning dramatically.
- Research the circumstances surrounding the writing of the piece.
- Read aloud – practicing variation in pace, pauses and emphasis.
- Practise reading and looking up regularly to allow more eye contact with the audience

Presentation

- Walk confidently and with poise to your reading position.
- Explain why you made your selection, the setting and any relevant information about the author.
- Use gestures to convey the mood, meaning and emotion.
- Variety in your voice such as pace, pitch, pause and volume will enhance the meaning.
- Hold your text in such a way that it does not hide your face and block your voice. If required use a music stand/lectern to rest it on.
- On conclusion wait for a few seconds before returning to your seat.

Chapter 21

Common Short Speeches

Introducing a Speaker

One of the most common speaking tasks is introducing a speaker – usually a special guest.

Introductions are basically a three step process:

1. Link the audience to subject (why should they be interested in this subject?)
2. Link the speaker to the subject (stating qualifications if appropriate)
3. Announce speaker's subject (or title of speech if used) and name

Beforehand

1. Check that you have the speaker's name, title and pronunciation correct. Make sure you have the speech/presentation title word perfect.
2. Consult the speaker who might have a number of things they would like mentioned beforehand - perhaps even a prepared introduction. If not, ask the question: "What can I say in my introduction that will help to make your presentation more successful?"

When You Speak

1. Be enthusiastic. Your job is to build the audience's anticipation for the speaker you are introducing.
2. Point out the relevance of the subject/speaker to this particular audience.
3. Build confidence by mentioning the speaker's qualifications to speak on a particular subject.
4. Generally, it creates more impact if the speaker's name is left till last.
5. Be brief - most introductions will only be a minute or so long.

Don't

1. Steal the speaker's impact. Don't give more subject matter than is necessary to build anticipation.
2. Try to upstage the speaker. The speaker is the "main act". Your job is to do everything possible to make this successful.
3. Forget to lead the applause.

A Not-So-Good Example

I'd like to introduce Nick Monsour the Personnel manager of Afgar Bank for his talk about the jobs going at his bank.

A Better Example

Banking and finance positions are some of the most highly sought after in our modern economy. Whether it's in the customer relations side or financial services there are excellent opportunities for skilled and dedicated workers. And there is no one better qualified than our guest to tell us all about these opportunities. He has been involved in the personnel side of banking for four years and so will be able to answer any questions you might have.

Please welcome the Personnel manager of Afgar bank, Nick Monsour.

The Vote of Thanks

Beforehand

1. Listen to the introduction. You may wish to comment on how the presentation fulfilled the promises made in the introduction.
2. Listen to the presentation. Try to note the one or two main points which impressed you.

When You Speak

1. Be specific. Without reiterating passages from the speech, try to mention how you were affected by particular points.
2. Be sincere. While your comments should generally be complimentary, insincere flattery is very transparent to an audience. Sometimes this calls for considerable diplomacy. You cannot say a presentation was "*really interesting*" if, in fact, it was quite boring. However, you could say "*it contained a great deal of important information*" or "*it showed that Mr Whitakker had gone to considerable trouble to prepare the relevant facts for us*".
3. Thank the speaker gracefully. Lead the applause and hand back to the Chairman, MC, etc.
4. Be brief.

A Not-So-Good Example

Thank you Mr Whitakker for coming and talking to us about our financial futures. I'm sure we all learned a great deal.

A Better Example

The world of work, money and how to secure our financial future are all important topics for young people. Today we have been fortunate to hear one of the experts in this field. Mr Neil Whitakker has certainly provided many helpful hints on how to increase our financial wealth. I thought *his advice on investing in managed share trusts particularly relevant. I am sure this has been* extremely beneficial talk for all concerned. Would you all join me in thanking Mr Whitakker for his efforts today.

The Speech of Congratulations

Beforehand

Make the effort to find out as much as you can about the recipient's area of expertise. What did it take for them to be receiving these congratulations?

When You Speak

Try to give the audience a feel of what the recipient had to go through to be deserving of the congratulations.

Remember to lead the applause.

STEP 1
The Award
Its selection criteria, the selectors/judges.
Its history – first awarded, past recipients.
Its significance – 'firsts' established by this win. (eg first winner from local area)

STEP 2
The Awardee
Any past awards – or is this the first?
Description of the dedication, skill, effort, etc required to win this award

STEP 3
The Presentation
Ask recipient to stand/come forward.
Lead applause with "Ladies & Gentlemen, lets' congratulate, the winner of the (year and name of award) – (recipient's name).

The Acceptance Speech (Winner)

Beforehand

Think about what you might say if you do win. Do this before you begin your preparation for the actual event.

When You Speak

Slow down – enjoy the moment. Let them see how happy/proud you are to win; but, don't let your exuberance cause you to say things or use language that you'll regret later.

STEP 1
What the win/award means to you
How long you've had this as your goal
How winning it makes you feel

STEP 2
Your winning strategy
What you did (differently/the same) that gave you the winning edge

STEP 3
Acknowledgements
Competitors
Past winners (inspiration)

STEP 4
Thank yous
Coach, team mates, officials
Support staff, supporters, family, friends

STEP 5
Where to from here
How winning this changes your opportunities/plans
What your goal(s) are now.

Prompt Phrases

- *Winning this has been my dream for....*
- *Right now I feel... (eg fantastic, proud, overwhelmed, grateful, find it hard to believe)*
- *What I think assisted me to win was...*
- *The competition was top class, so I'd like to acknowledge all those who made this such a great contest.*
- *I'd also like to thank (past winner(s) who was an inspiration to me.*

The Acceptance Speech (Runner-Up)

Beforehand

Enquire about whether a runner-up speech is required. If so, think about what you might say . Do this before you begin your preparation for the actual event.

When You Speak

Be gracious and grateful. Try not to let your disappointment at not winning show. Keep it brief.

STEP 1
Congratulate the winner (if known)
Specify one attribute that contributed to their win

STEP 2
What you'd do differently/the same next time.
What you did (differently/the same) that gave you the winning edge

STEP 3
Acknowledgements
Competition

STEP 4
Thankyous
Coach, team mates, officials
Support staff, supporters, family, friends
Sponsors

STEP 5
Where to from here
How this placing changes your opportunities/plans
What your goal(s) are now.

Prompt Phrases

- *Firstly, I'd like to congratulate (the winner).*
- *What was so impressive about (the winner) throughout the contest was his/her...*
- *If I were to do anything differently next time, I think it would be...*
- *The competition was top class, so I'd like to acknowledge all those who made this such a great contest.*
- *I'd also like to thank (past winner(s)) who was an inspiration to me.*

Chapter 22

The Persuasive Presentation

A persuasive presentation is a speaker attempting to move their listeners to action. The underlying principle is that people are most likely to act when they understand clearly the benefits they will derive from it.

The Formula IPASCAPE provides an easy-to-apply format that will suit any persuasive presentation

The 8 Steps are -

Interests

It is important to show that the speaker understands what is important to the group they are speaking to. This might be something very general: "*I know that breathing clean air is something that's important to you.*" Or, it may be quite specific: "*Everyone in this class is looking forward to our trip to the National Capital next month.*"

Problem

The problem is defined clearly and succinctly. It is best for the speaker to be inclusive ("***We** have a problem...*") rather than accusatory ("***You** have a problem*").

Affect

The way that this problem will affect this group. This is, most often, a 'tie-back' to the opening 'Interests' statement.

Solution

As soon as the problem has been fully explained, the speaker needs to provide what they believe is the solution – or, at least, part of the solution. The speaker clarified how this problem will affect this group in particular, so any solution will involve this group doing something to help solve it.

Cost

Any solution is going to involve a cost. This may be in monetary terms, but is just as likely to be changed behaviour and/or a shift in attitude.

Advantages

This is where the speaker 'sells' the solution and justifies the cost by explaining what's in it for them to change the way the speaker is suggesting. This gives the speaker to use their descriptive and/or storytelling skills to powerfully articulate the benefit(s) they will gain.

Point to Start

The speaker is most likely to be successful if they make it easy for their listeners to act as they ask. Break what they need to do down into small steps and make the first step easy.

Encourage

This is where the speaker finishes on a high note. This is best done by painting a picture in the audience's mind of how much better things will be in the future. This is known as the 'assumed close' i.e. the speaker assumes that the audience will do as they request

Here are exemplars of two typical persuasive presentations.

	Speech 1	Speech 2
PURPOSE	*To persuade a group to help improve air quality*	*To persuade a group to better support a fundraising drive*
INTEREST	*"We all love to breathe clean air."*	*"Everyone in this class is looking forward to our trip to the national capital next semester."*
PROBLEM	*"The way our city is increasing in population, air pollution will become an increasing problem."*	*"Unfortunately, the fundraising has been going very poorly. This means that we won't have enough money to pay for the expenses."*
AFFECT	*"This will affect the quality of life for us all. Obviously, those who suffer breathing difficulties are at most risk; but, we're all affected by it. There's nothing worse that looking out and seeing that horrible smog that blankets our city when the conditions are wrong."*	*"So if this happens, our parents are going to be asked to put in much more money. Some students might not be able to go."*
SOLUTION	*"One way to improve the situation, is for us to cut down on the number of car journeys we take. If we could reduce this by just 10%, it would make a massive difference to the quality of air in our city.*	*"There is still five weeks to go, and if we can really pick up with selling those fundraising chocolates – and sell all those in the deputy principal's office – we will get the money we need."*
COST	*"Yes there will be a cost. It is less convenient to catch a bus or train than ask mum or dad to drive you. It takes more effort to walk or ride a bike. You have to be more organised to use public transport."*	*"Sure, this will cost you. No, I'm not expecting you to buy the chocolates yourself. We have been given a stand at the local Sunday markets. I want you to volunteer some of your time over the next five Sundays to sell our chocolates at the markets."*
ADVANTAGES	*"The cost will be worth it because you will be helping to keep our city a great place to live. You'll feel better about yourself, your parents will appreciate your efforts and you'll get fitter!"*	*"If we all put our names down, you'll only need to be there for half-a-day on one Sunday. It'll be fun being at the markets – and we're sure to sell all the chocolates; so our trip can go ahead!*
POINT to START	*"So, here's how you can get started straight away. Think of just one occasion a week when you could get yourself somewhere – by public transport, bike or walking – instead of having someone drive you. Start next week."*	*All I need you to do is put your name down on this roster I have – just one half-day...it's easy.*
ENCOURAGE	*"This might seem like such a little thing to do, but if we all just do a little bit, it makes a huge difference. And that has to make you breathe easier"*	*"It's only five weeks and we'll all be hopping on that plane. It's going to be great; so put your name down and help us get there!"*

A persuasive presentation can be delivered following the IPASCASE formula in 3 to 4 minutes.

Their test speech may be given to –

- Their fellow students as an audience. This should be the easiest type of presentation because of their awareness of the group's interests and attitudes.
- A hypothetical audience. This is a greater challenge because they need to do audience research.

While the first is an excellent starting point, the second provides greater learning for the student.

Possible Persuasive Presentation Topics

Support a worthy cause
Try out a new/unusual sport or activity
Attend a particular event
Stand up against bullying
Watch a new/unusual television show or movie
Visit a particular place
Support a particular team
Try out a particular restaurant/cuisine
Purchase a product
Join a particular group
Read a certain book – or just read more books
Use your time more wisely/effectively (eg play less computer games)
Improve your fitness and/or diet
Plan to avoid stress
Take every opportunity – everything worthwhile is scary
Make time for those who mean most to you
Listen to a different type of music
Work to stop an ongoing injustice
Be a better son/daughter/student and/or friend
See a problem as an opportunity
Don't be a hypocrite – saying one thing and acting differently
Giving is better than receiving
Money doesn't bring happiness
Change the flag
There are more important things than wearing the right designer brands
Choose the words you say with care
Stand up for yourself and your values – don't bow to peer pressure
It's great to have something to be proud of
In a changing world some traditions are good
You enjoy something so much more if you've earned it

The Persuasive Presentation

Interests

It is important to show that the speaker understands what is important to the group they are speaking to. This might be something very general: "*I know that breathing clean air is something that's important to you.*"

Or, it may be quite specific: "*Everyone in this class is looking forward to our trip to the National Capital next month.*"

Problem

The problem is defined clearly and succinctly. It is best for the speaker to be inclusive :"***We** have a problem...*" rather than accusatory "***You** have a problem.*"

Affect

The way that this problem will affect this group. This is, most often, a 'tie-back' to the opening 'Interests' statement.

Solution

As soon as the problem has been fully explained, the speaker needs to provide what they believe is the solution - or, at least, part of the solution. The speaker clarified how this problem will affect this group in particular, so any solution will involve this group doing something to help solve it.

Cost

Any solution is going to involve a cost. This may be in monetary terms, but is just as likely to be changed behaviour and/or a shift in attitude.

Advantages

This is where the speaker 'sells' the solution and justifies the cost by explaining what's in it for them to change the way the speaker is suggesting. This gives the speaker to use their descriptive and/or storytelling skills to powerfully articulate the benefit(s) they will gain.

Point to Start

The speaker is most likely to be successful if they make it easy for their listeners to act as they ask. Break what they need to do down into small steps and make the first step easy.

Encourage

This is where the speaker finishes on a high note. This is best done by painting a picture in the audience's mind of how much better things will be in the future. This is known as the 'assumed close' i.e. the speaker assumes that the audience will do as they request

Chapter 23

The Informative Oral

Purpose

One of the most common speeches presented is that which tells the audience something they will find helpful and worthwhile to add to their knowledge base. Opportunities for the informative speech are many. They occur wherever reports are being made, instructional material is being presented or ideas being delivered by means of lectures or discussions.

Definition

The speech to inform people provides them with a clear understanding of the speaker's ideas about a topic. It creates interest in the topic because the material that is presented is relevant to the listeners.

Requirements

This oral can be taught by breaking up the process into a number of stages.

Stage 1: Type of Approach

The purpose of this stage is to have the students consider what type of approach they will take in preparing their informative oral.

This approach will be determined by:

- the purpose - if it is to inform the audience about a particular event or process, the speaker might use a Documentary
- the audience and the occasion - a humorous approach would probably not be suitable for a speech about youth suicide
- the speaker's own skills and personality - these have a good deal of bearing on which approach is chosen.

Emphasise that an original approach will make their oral presentation more interesting to write, more engaging to listen to and will be more likely to be delivered confidently.

Stage 2: Support Material

Points to make to the students:

- Organise their material into clear manageable parts and present these in a logical order.
- Give explanations. For every main point made an example, an illustration, a story or an image should be included.
- Include a mixture of facts. As this an Informative Oral a great deal of your material should come from your research. Look for interesting ways to include the material.

Stage 3 Using Notes

Ask students to fill in:

- the purpose of their speech
- the message of their speech
- the two or three points they will talk about
- the support material they will use for each of their points.

If there is time, have them share this information with fellow students (in pairs or small groups) for them to get reassurance that the material is interesting.

Stage 4: Using Aids

Use props, visual aids, humour, examples, quotes, stories, drama or intriguing material to ensure your presentation is interesting.

Revisit the information on Body Language and Visual Aids.

Stage 5: Preparing to Deliver

Controlling Nerves

Nervousness is natural. Eliminating it altogether is probably impossible but it CAN be controlled.

Be convinced and care about your message. The principle is that the more we care about the audience really getting our message, the less we focus on what they are thinking of us.

The last five minutes

Review the Chapter 'Speaking to a Group'. Tell your students that they can do this well and will have the chance to practise the mental and physical preparation.

The last check

Before students commence their presentations, remind and encourage them to check any details with you beforehand.

exercises

1. Conduct a class exercise with a hypothetical speech -

   '(Insert your school name here) - One of this Country's Great Schools'

   Work through the various types of approaches. Ask students if they can think of any other approaches. Identify how you could use each of the 7 approaches for the hypothetical speech

   Examples -

   i. Dramatisation - Describe the scene on the school's first day, or a great moment in the school's history.
   ii. Documentary - Similar to above, but imagine you're a journalist from the local Newspaper at the school's opening, or a current affairs TV reporter.
   iii. Allegorical Approach - Compare the school's history to other organizations or institutions eg a family, a tribe
   iv. Role Play - Play the role of a parent deciding where to send their child to school.
   v. Humour - Tell the history of the school in terms of funny incidents that have happened over the years.
   vi. Shock/Horror - Start with names of past students and teachers who have died. Talk about how they added to the school's spirit..
   vii. Emotional - Make other students proud to share in such a rich history

2. This lesson is to show students that there some structures they can use that will lead to a good Informative Oral.

   Have the students read the Exemplar: **A Great Speech So Much More than Words.**

   Then look at the diagram on page 88 in the Informative Oral Information Sheet and have the students fill in the example space with brief notes from the text of **A Great Speech So Much More Than Words.** They should be able to find the Purpose, an Outline, First Point etc

Exemplar – Defining a Concept

A Great Speech – So Much More than Words

What makes a great speech? It's not just clever words. It's not just a scintillating speaker. It seems to need both of these – and more. I believe a great speech can be defined by three elements – Timing, Attention and Connection; and I'd like to explain these one-by-one.

Firstly, timing. Great speeches are not so much about saying the right thing, but saying the right thing at the right time. Speeches exist 'in the moment' – a great speech given at a different time loses impact. Martin Luther King delivered one of the greatest speeches of all time - 'I Have a Dream' - to large civil rights rallies in the 1960s. Imagine this speech given at a different place and different time – hardly the same effect!

When the World Trade Centre Towers in New York were attacked, the President, George W Bush, went on national television. In his speech he said – "Today, our nation saw evil, the very worst of human nature, and we responded with the best of America, with the daring of our rescue workers, with the caring for strangers and neighbours who came to give blood and help in any way they could." This was exactly what the American people needed to hear at the time. A positive, uplifting message to a sad, shocked nation. This is what made it a great speech – it's timing. George W Bush has given many speeches about that terrible event since then, but none have worked as well as the one he gave on the evening of 11 September 2001.

So you can't ever know if a speech is great by just reading – or even listening to – the words. You also have to know something about who is being spoken to and the circumstances at the time.

The second element of a great speech is attention – a great speech grabs and holds an audience's attention throughout. It might do this with wise words or the way the speaker says it – or something else. And it has to get you attention with something that makes you think. A big blockbuster movie can entertain you with explosions, car crashes and amazing visual effects – but unless it has a good message; you've forgotten about it soon after you leave the theatre. A great speech is like a great movie – it holds your attention all the way through – and still has you thinking about it days later.

So far, I've covered timing and attention. Now for the most difficult to explain – the third element that I call connection. A great speech is one where the speaker really connects with the audience – they are really involved in the speech, they relate to everything that is said, they really get it.

The best way I've heard it described is that it's like two cliffs separated by a deep gorge. The speaker and their message is on one cliff, and the audience is on the other cliff. A good speech 'connects' these two by building 'bridges'. These 'bridges' are what a good speaker adds to help the audience relate to and understand what is being said.

A good example of this is when a lot of statistics and figures are quoted in a speech – especially when the numbers are big. I can't relate to how many a billion is, how far a light years is, how big 100,000 square kilometers is. If I'm told that 150,000 square kilometers of rainforest is destroyed every year, it means little to me. But if it's described as the equivalent of nine football fields of rainforest every minute of every hour of every day…I can understand the extent of the problem.

Another great way to connect with an audience is to tell a story. And the best stories are those that the speaker actually experienced. Audiences love stories, and they feel really involved if they can 'connect' with one of the characters in the story – the speaker.

I've listened to and read many, many speeches in researching this presentation. Some of them were great, some pretty ordinary, and some were truly awful. But, the common ingredients in all the great speeches were timing, attention and connection.

Informative Orals – Typical Speeches

- Describing a place, person, group, organisation, activity, process or event
- Defining a concept, principle or ideal. Examples: jazz or rap (as opposed to other music styles), responsible citizenship, honesty, discrimination, the welfare state, democracy, open-mindedness.

Here are some suggestions-

Place	Planet (other than Earth) Country/Region City (Present or Past) National Park/Wilderness	Point of Interest Museum/Gallery Building Theme Park	Holiday Destination Prison/Detention Centre Stadium Lookout/Viewing Point
Person	Political Figure Head of State Sporting Great Philanthropist	Great Scientist Great Composer/Artist Great Military Leader Business Leader	Philosopher/Teacher Religious Leader Adventurer Entertainer
Group	School 'House' Club Musical Group Sporting Team	Family Social Group Common Interest Group Support Group	Debating Team Holiday Group Volunteers Research Group
Organisation	Government/Parliament United Nations 'G7' Group of Nations Political Party	OPEC OECD Red Cross/Crescent Amnesty International	Greenpeace Care International ACTU FIFA/NRL/AFL/NBL
Activity	Sport Playing Music Chess/Bridge Reading/Writing	Collecting (eg stamps) Computer Games Charity Work Graphic Arts	Cooking Part-time job Scouting, Bushwalking Gardening
Process	Factory Lawmaking Computer Processing Training Program (eg Dreamweaver)	Buying a home theatre Planning an overseas trip Auditioning for a TV show Learning to ride a bike/ horse	Making model planes/candles/ Archaeological Dig Growing hydroponic vegetables Building a shed/fence/pool
Event	Historical Event Anniversary Big Day Out/Concert Melbourne Cup	Grand Final Yacht Race Anzac Day Family Celebration	Funeral Exhibition/Art Show Parade Market
Concept	Welfare State Perpetual Motion Baby Boomer/Gen Y Capitalism	Socialism Anarchy Reincarnation Democracy	Success Happiness The Global Village Genetic Engineering
Principle/ Ideal	Fairness Equality Honesty Open-Mindedness	Mateship Loyalty Bravery Justice	Teamwork Responsible Citizenship Empathy/Understanding Free Trade

THE INFORMATIVE ORAL

Stage 1: Type of Approach

Your approach will be determined by:

- The purpose - if it is to inform the audience about a particular event or process, you might use a Documentary.
- The audience and the occasion - a humorous approach would probably not be suitable for a speech about youth suicide.
- Your own skills and personality - these have a good deal of bearing on which approach is chosen.
- An original approach will make your oral presentation more interesting to write, more engaging to listen to and will be easier to be deliver confidently.

Stage 2: Support Material

- Organise your material into clear manageable parts and present these in a logical order.
- Give explanations. For every main point made an example, an illustration, a story or an image should be included.
- Include a mixture of facts. As this an Informative Oral a great deal of your material should come from your research. Look for interesting ways to include the material.

Stage 3 Using Notes

- Notes that allow you to look at the audience

Stage 4: Using Aids

Use props, visual aids, humour, examples, quotes, stories, drama or intriguing material to ensure your presentation is interesting.

Stage 5: Preparing to Deliver

Controlling Nerves

Nervousness is natural. Eliminating it altogether is probably impossible but it CAN be controlled.

Be convinced and care about your message. The principle is that the more we care about the audience really getting our message, the less we focus on what they are thinking of us.

Chapter 24

The Reflective Oral

The reflective oral complements and develops many aspects of the earlier work you would have done on conversations. Story telling and impromptu speaking.

Stage 1 **Overview**

This is a series of activities that will culminate in the presentation of a Reflective Oral Assignment. Students will –

1. review the principles of an effective speech.
2. choose the topic for a reflective oral
3. write a presentation and hand it in to demonstrate the use of speech writing techniques
4. present the reflective oral to the class to be assessed.

Stage 2 **Definition and Topic**

Students will, ideally, have a fairly clear idea about their intended topic and approach by the end of this activity. Suggestions:

- *an occasion or event that had an unexpected outcome*
- *a person you met (or whom you know) who has influenced you.*

The Reflective Oral – a Definition

A Reflective Oral consists of the speaker looking back on an experience (event, period of time or other influencing factor) and 'reflecting' on how this affected them. It is a personal reflection; so it not only tells the audience about the experience; but it also includes personal insights to the speaker's thoughts and feelings and how this affected their opinion, attitude or behaviour.

It demonstrates all the components of an effective speech in both content and delivery.

Introduce the activity by having four or five students deliver a one minute Impromptu Speech. These are designed to give the students further experience of speaking in front of a group and with a topic that has some close link to the eventual type of presentation students will be asked to present

To help the students work on their reflective story telling skills, use topics that require them to recount an incident and explain how it affected them.

For example:

- *Tell us about a tough time you have faced in your life – and how it changed you.*
- *Tell us about the most famous person you have met – and the effect they had on you.*

Stage 3 **Topic Selection**

Reflective Orals often contain stories and almost always involve descriptive speaking; so being skilled in these areas is important for successful Reflective Oral presentations.

Suitable topics for a Reflective Oral might be –

- *A travel experience and how it changed you.*
- *Your proudest/happiest/saddest/most embarrassing experience and how you remember it now.*

- *A person you know/have known and the influence they had on you.*
- *A particular period of your life – what it was like living through it and what you think of that time now.*
- *A famous news event (eg 9/11) – what you were doing at the time and how it affected you.*
- *An event that changed the way you think or behave.*

Continue the practice of having four or five students deliver a one minute Impromptu Speech. These are designed to give the students further experience of speaking in front of a group and with a topic that has some close link to the eventual type of presentation students will be asked to present

Stage 4 **Telling the Story**

Revisit the Story Telling Chapter (page 53)

Story-Telling consists of 4 steps –

1. Background/Set-Up Information
2. Describe Scene
3. Introduce Characters
4. Describe Action (Including Dialogue)

Identify the elements of a good story (with suggestions from the class). These include

- *characters the audience can relate to*
- *vivid scene description (& if necessary, background to the story)*
- *fast-moving action that the audience can easily follow*
- *realistic dialogue*
- *overcoming adversity*
- *direct link to the speaker*

Stage 5 **The Reflection Process**

Assist the students' reflection by examining the following questions.

- *How important was it to you at the time?*
- *How important is it to you now?*
- *How did you feel about it then?*
- *How do you feel about it in hindsight? (Feelings involved might include happiness, remorse, regret, satisfaction, relief, gladness, shame, embarrassment, resignation, gratitude, resentment, determination, anger, pride)*
- *Has anything like this ever happened to you (or someone you know) before?*
- *What might you have done differently?*
- *How might it have turned out differently?*
- *How did it change the way you think, feel and/or act?*

Have students create the structure of their Reflective Oral by listing (in bullet point form)

- *the descriptive elements of the Oral (story, person, etc)*
- *the reflective* elements of the story (based on the list above – but not limited to it).

If time allows, have students share their 'draft' presentations in small groups (4-5).

Presentation Summary/Worksheet

Opening

Descriptive Content

Reflective Content

Conclusion

Possible Impromptu Topics for Students

My Happiest Experience (at home/at school/on the sporting field)

My Saddest Experience (at home/at school/on the sporting field)

My Most Exciting Adventure

My Greatest Embarrassment (at home/at school/on the sporting field)

An Amazing Coincidence

Reaching a Goal

The Day I Learned an Important Lesson

My First Day at School

My Favourite Teacher in Primary (& why she/he was)

Experiencing My First Big Win

Experiencing My First Real Defeat

The Scariest Moment in My Life

I Thought I Was Going to Die

The Holiday/Excursion That Didn't Go as Planned

The Funniest Thing that's Ever Happened to Me

It Must Have Been Aliens

My Proudest Moment (at home/school/on the sporting field)

How We Became Best Friends

An Incident I'll Remember Until I Die

Chapter 25

The Film Review

A film review can be a very worthwhile opportunity to have students speak about something that is within their experience. By using the INFORMATION SHEET provided as a discussion guide with your students you can be sure they are covering all the necessary steps for creating a worthwhile presentation.

The next section is important in making students aware that their oral presentations need to be more than a written essay that they read to their audience. Students should spend time on the following :

- the differences between the **Written Word** and the **Spoken Word**.
- speakers use shorter words.
- speakers will use repetition for emphasis whereas writers avoid repetition.
- speakers keep sentences as short as possible, while writers tend to write longer sentences that can be quite complex.
- speakers use a conversational language. Contractions are OK for example.
- speakers know that the sounds of words contribute to their meaning. How easy a word is to pronounce may affect its choice.

The Main Points

Discuss plot, Setting, Theme, Characters, Dialogue

Emphasise that this a spoken presentation and not a written review. Therefore different style elements are required.

exercises

1. Imagine you are a reporter for a television variety show aimed at teenagers. Using the film you watched, prepare a 4 to 5 minute review for your viewing audience.

   Your talk should:

   - *Give your opinion of the film*
   - *Mention all the key elements of a film- plot, theme, characters, dialogue, setting and film techniques.*
   - *Mention an interesting or exciting part of the film.*
   - *Evaluate the film*

   Your aim is to inform and entertain the viewer about the film. You need a balance of description and evaluation to do this.

1. You are a well-known film producer and have been invited to address a group of students who have studied your film as part of their English course. As your time with these students will mostly be a question and answer session, your introductory talk of 4-5minutes needs to be an overview of the film including:

   - *central issue/s that you wanted to convey*
   - *how you used your characters to convey your messages*
   - *what film techniques you used to create a memorable film*

what you need to know about...

FRAMEWORK OF IDEAS FOR A FILM REVIEW

PLOT

- outline briefly the main events of the story.
- what type of film is it? To what genre (horror, western, comedy) does it belong?
- comment on the sorts of emotions the film makers were trying to create (consider dramatic tension, conflict)?
- comment on the subjects/topics which the film examines?
- comment on the film structure.
- consider humour (if there is any) of dialogue, character, description, situation.
- comment on any special effects used for impact?

SETTING

- are the settings and the costumings appropriate for the film?
- in what period of time is the story set?
- are there any flashbacks or any big leaps in time?

THEME

- what message was the film maker trying to convey?

CHARACTERS

- consider the casting and performances of the actors.
- how many of the characters are explored in depth?
- what are their personalities, feelings, strengths, weaknesses and relationships to others?
- does the film emphasize character or is it more concerned with action or visual interest?

DIALOGUE

- how much dialogue is there?
- is it natural or designed for effect?
- how do the individual characters speak?
- does their speech distinguish them from other characters?

OTHER ASPECTS

A good review comments on a variety of aspects. Try to find out the names of the director, producer, scriptwriter, director of photography and the names of the main actors. You may be able to mention previous work by them.

CONCLUSION

- sum up by giving your general impression of the film—why you liked it or disliked it.
- what aspects of it seemed outstanding or lacking?
- consider the performances of the actors.
- consider camera work, lighting, editing. Has the editing achieved the right pace and placed shots in the most effective way.
- what is the quality of the soundtrack? Has the mix of dialogue, music and natural sounds been of high quality?

Chapter 26

The Oral and Shakespeare

A popular and common area of study is Shakespeare and the tasks below refer to some specific types of orals that could be presented. It may also be applicable to a novel or play that you have taught. Tasks Three and Four in particular deal with a Eulogy and although the task applies to Shakespeare, it could also be used in any work of literature which has the death of one of the major characters.

Other types of Shakespearean orals could be as follows:

Task One

Shakespeare's plays highlight a variety of aspects of human nature. They deal with good, evil, corruption, greed as well as the fallible nature of human beings. This is one reason why his works continue to be popular.

Ask students to present a talk to assist future students of Shakespeare by praising the virtues of studying " *Hamlet* ". The talk will be placed on tape as part of a kit for students entering Senior English. The kit will be titled " *All You Need To Know* " and is designed to prepare and advise them for their final year of English study.

In the talk the people as well as the issues which make the play worthy of study should be highlighted..

Task Two

The task is to talk to a group of young adult readers and discuss the benefits of studying a Shakespearean play. In the talk students might consider the following:

- *the characters and what we learn from them.*
- *the themes and their relevance to the 21st century.*
- *the language and how the imagery contributes to the play.*
- *why Shakespeare's work is still popular today.*

Task Three: HAMLET

As a result of the Ghost's request of Hamlet to avenge his father's death, a number of prominent members of the Royal Court of Denmark died. The task is to choose a role and a personality from the box below, and deliver the eulogy at the funeral service of one of these prominent personalities. The speech should take 5-6 minutes.

The audience is the surviving members and mourners of the Royal Court of Denmark.

NB. The role chosen must be appropriate for the personality, ie. Polonius couldn't deliver a eulogy for Laertes.

ROLE	PERSONALITY
Fortinbras	Claudius
Horatio	Hamlet
Osric	Laertes
Laertes	Polonius

Task Four: JULIUS CAESAR

As a result of the struggle for power, in the Shakespearian play Julius Caesar, a number of prominent Romans die. Your task is to choose a role and a personality from the box below, and deliver the eulogy at the funeral service of one of these prominent personalities. You've been allocated 5-6 minutes for your speech.

ROLE	**PERSONALITY**
Brutus	Portia
A Citizen	Julius Caesar
Casca	Cassius
Antony	Brutus

CRITERIA	**SPECIFIC COMMENTS**
CONTENT: indicates chosen Role and Personality clearly; outlines Personality's status/position, character traits, personal qualities, mentions faults; praises their accomplishments; Length 5-6 minutes.	
STRUCTURE: Organised logically; possessing an identifiable Intro, Body and Conclusion; Balanced; Cohesive and unified piece of work.	
LANGUAGE: Formal and appropriate for nominated audience; Informative; Praiseworthy; dignified; solemn; Explanatory; Vocabulary appropriate to the task.	
PRESENTATION: Manipulation of voice features - audibility, clarity, pace, intonation; Manipulation of non-verbal features - gestures, facial expression, eye-contact, movement.	

Here Is a Sample Marking Sheet For The Eulogy Task.

GENERAL COMMENT: ____

____

____

MARKER: ____________________________

DATE: ____________________________

The Eulogy

A Eulogy is a formal dignified speech, or piece of writing, which praises a person or thing.

A Eulogy is also known as a funeral speech and is most often delivered by a friend, relative or colleague at the funeral service of the deceased.

CONTENT

- the audience must be able to recognize that what you say is honest.
- the audience must be able to relate to the qualities that you mention.
- outline the good points of the deceased—in their character, their personality traits, in the way they related to other people, in their actions.
- mention some of the weaknesses in order to maintain the honesty and integrity of both the speaker and deceased.
- a touch of humour may be added if its purpose is to illustrate something of the life of the person.
- if the manner of death has been a violent one, it is not usually mentioned but accepted as common knowledge.

STRUCTURE

- the introduction conveys the full name and other relevant personal information is conveyed.
- the body of the speech expands upon the qualities of the person.
- the conclusion ends the eulogy with public thanks for the life of the deceased.

Hints

- keep it simple
- select appropriate words.
- plan the order of content.
- be logical.
- use a tone of voice suited to the occasion ie. dignified and solemn.

An example of a eulogy to "Hamlet"

Hamlet, Prince of Denmark, son of the late King Hamlet and son of the late Queen Gertrude. In life and through his tragic death he was a man who affected us all and his tale is one which history shall never forget. We are gathered here today to remember and give thanks for the life of a truly remarkable man As I recall the life of our beloved Prince, there are three things that strike me about Hamlet. Firstly his diversity and depth of character. Secondly , his accomplishment of being a most noble prince and thirdly, his widespread popularity.

Hamlet was a passionate man who followed his heart in decision and action. He pursued his interests keenly. He excelled in the academic world of the University of Wittenburg. He was an outstanding exponent in the field of fencing and he had a passion for the stage. He was indeed a well rounded man. As Ophelia said, "*he was the glass of fashion and mould of form.*"

How would I describe the character of Hamlet? Hamlet the melancholic, compassionate, noble, troubled, loving, reflective, and sensitive Prince of Denmark. For those of you who knew Hamlet would be able to relate to the fact that he was a very diverse and complicated character. But amongst this complexity and amongst any faults was a truly remarkable human being.

Hamlet loved his parents, his care and affection for them could not be overcome. The court witnessed his sincere grief when Hamlet lost his father. He was obedient to his mother , "I shall in all my best obey you madam" is how he would often reply to his mother's requests. In truth Hamlet was an extremely sensitive person. His nature was philosophical, reflective, prone to questioning and therefore Hamlet was influenced by the greater moral implications of any act.

As well as being an accomplished prince, Hamlet was also a well loved and popular prince. His death is not only a great loss for the royal court but also for all of Denmark. As Claudius remarked: "He's loved of the distracted multitude". Hamlet's popularity with his people sprung from his ability to relate to all types of people. He could converse with grave diggers, to players and to the general populace. Furthermore, Hamlet was respected in noble circles. Fortinbras, the Prince of Norway had four captains bear Hamlet onto a stage and shoot a peal of ordnance as a sign of respect. Hamlet's character, his nobility, and his popularity were the three attributes which made him such a remarkable man.

However Hamlet was never strong or forceful by nature and it was this inability to act on what his heart felt which led to his demise. Hamlet was never one to be violent or vindictive and thus when faced with the dilemma of having to avenge his father's death, could not do it. This was certainly a dark stage in Hamlet's life. His cruel treatment of Ophelia, his remorseless, ruthless treatment of Rosencrantz and Guildenstern and his satirical teasing of Polonius all stemmed from this disillusionment he felt towards life. How I wish it had not been so.

However we must not remember Hamlet merely because of the difficult circumstances he faced towards the end of his life nor his tragic death. We remember him for the remarkable human being he was and the noble prince he became. And when he died a noble heart did crack. *Goodnight sweet prince and flights of angels sing thee to thy rest.*

Chapter 27

The Radio Talk

Radio speaking presents a different way to extend the abilities of students. When they perform on radio they need to create a friendly, conversational style and have material that immediately catches and holds the listeners' attention.

exercises

Introductory Activity for Students

Record a selection of different segments that can be listened to on radio.

For example, news reports, weather reports, station breaks, commercials, song introductions, feature programs.

Ask students to identify these speaking situations that they hear when listening to their favourite radio station and answer the following questions.

- What was the particular segment that they heard?
- How long was it?
- What type of language was used?
- How did the announcer make the segment interesting to listen to?

The Rules of Radio

Students will come to appreciate certain speaking rules need to apply when they start to prepare a segment for presentation..

Organisation:

- Use a simple plan of how your radio talk would be structured.
- Numbering of your points if necessary.
- Keep your sentences short to make it easier to listen to. A general rule is to keep your sentences to about 20 words or less.

Capture the attention of listeners by using a variety of devices.

- Use repetition to reinforce your ideas.
- Use examples that are new, unusual or show contrast.
- Use action verbs to keep your ideas sounding interesting.

Microphone Techniques

- An effective radio speaker needs to achieve the spontaneity and liveliness of conversation.
- Students should be encouraged to imagine they are speaking to just one or two friends.
- An effective speaker needs to use all the techniques of oral interpretation.

Volume: Keep this constant. Don't fade at the end of sentences.

Articulation: Words need to be understood by the audience otherwise they will turn you off.

Pace: A normal speaking rate is about 135 words per minute. Don't rush.

Gestures and Facial Expressions: Don't be afraid to use them. They won't be seen but they will be heard. Proper gestures will give your voice believability.

exercises

Radio Presentation Skills

1. Have students prepare a 30 second commercial. Use examples from current radio commercials. Choice of a product or service can be up to the student.
2. Ask your students to prepare a Station break. Possible scenarios could be:

   Hip hop radio station

   Country and western station

   Popular music station

   Station playing hits from the 70's and 80's
3. Ask your students to prepare a Public service announcement.

   This is could be a weather warning about a possible thunderstorm coming soon.

   It could be an appeal to support a particular organisation which is holding a doorknock appeal eg Salvation Army Red Shield Appeal.
4. Ask your students to write a short news item and present it.
5. Ask your students to listen to a weather report on a station and then write and present their own weather report.
6. A Radio Presentation -- this puts together all the skills your students have been practising in the previous Exercises.

   Divide the class into groups and ask them to write, rehearse and broadcast a ten minute radio program.

   Give them a set format. Here is a possible format.

   Radio Presentation Format

(10sec)	Station Break Announce the time Identify the station name
(1min)	Public Service Announcement (Do only one) *Give to a charity organisation* *Vote at an election* *Attend* an event
(1min)	Commercial Use two voices and one sound effect
(2min)	News Use all of the following: International, national, state and local
(2min)	Sports News International, national, state and local
(1min)	Weather report and forecast
(30sec)	Commercial
(2min)	Feature Program Some ideas could include: *Interview with a celebrity* *Talk* about an upcoming concert
(10 sec)	Sign Off

7. The Radio Play

   A radio play offers students the opportunity for greater self expression than a debate or speech. It can build confidence and show students the range of problems this type of speaking activity can produce.

   A radio play is a dramatic production for broadcast. It is characterised by sound effects, musical background, and little if any stage action by the participants.

exercises

Selecting a play

- Choose radio plays from the library resources.
- Alternatively read examples of plays and look to edit, rewrite or cut significant parts out of the play.
- Alternatively students could be encouraged to write their own scripts.

Preparation

- Choose the casts carefully. Four or five persons are a manageable number. In casting it is recommended that different style voices be used to allow listeners to identify them more easily.
- Sound effects may need a great deal of work to obtain the desired effect.
- Co-ordination of all the characters, sound effects, music and announcing is vital.
- The mechanics of production are essential. Distance from the microphone, rustling of papers clearing of the throat and incorrect reading are all elements to be avoided.
- Rehearse with a tape recorder to improve your overall performance.

Presentation

- Characters must come to life with the naturalness of the speaker.
- Timing is vital if the play is to have a clarity and impact.
- Clear pronunciation aids the overall effect of the production.
- Use gestures and facial expressions. They won't be seen but they will be heard. Proper gestures will give a sense of 'believability' to your voice.

Hints

Imagine you are presenting your talk to possibly small groups of people who are listening. This means your voice needs to have enough clarity, volume and vibrancy to give interest.

If you feel like gesturing, do so. It will add life to your speech.

Rehearse with a live microphone to be fully prepared.